Your Advertising's Great...
Great...
How's Business?

The Revolution In Sales Promotion

Your Advertising's Great. . . How's Business?

The Revolution In Sales Promotion

Bud Frankel
Frankel & Company

H. W. Phillips
Purdue University

DOW JONES-IRWIN   Homewood, Illinois   60430

This publication is designed to provide accurate and
authoritative information in regard to the subject matter
covered. It is sold with the understanding that neither the
authors nor the publisher is engaged in rendering legal, accounting,
or other professional service. If legal advice or other expert
assistance is required, the services of a competent
professional person should be sought.

*From a Declaration of Principles jointly adopted by a Committee
of the American Bar Association and a Committee of Publishers.*

ISBN 0-87094-543-2

Library of Congress Catalog Card No. 85-72254

Printed in the United States of America

2 3 4 5 6 7 8 9 0 DO 3 2 1 0 9 8 7 6

Preface

More than 10 years have passed since marketing statistics first revealed that sales promotion expenditures were consistently exceeding those of advertising. By 1976, many marketers had become acutely aware of how their promotion dollars were being spent. They began to realize that they could no longer view their sales promotion (nonmedia) and advertising (media) efforts as mutually exclusive activities.

Up until that time, *nonmedia marketing* seemed to be a contradiction in terms. The term *marketing,* to the contrary, was synonymous with media purchases, advertising exclusively; all other efforts in the marketplace were viewed as afterthoughts.

In recent years, however, more and more marketers have not only broadened their marketing definitions (to include everything from packaging, to pricing, to promotion, to direct mail, to telemarketing), but they have also changed and broadened their actual marketing strategies and structures. If they are to achieve their marketing objectives, marketers must realize that a balance of media and nonmedia activities is necessary to create an action-effective marketing mix.

Even though such strategy is neither true of all marketers' programs nor recommended by numerous marketing texts, the vast majority of Fortune 500 companies now have separate departments designed specifically for nonmedia marketing; and those departments are growing, both in size and in responsibilities. (This trend has also given birth to innumerable nonadvertising agencies involved in sales promotion, marketing services, and direct marketing.)

Marketers' changing and continually developing perspective on nonmedia marketing is a primary reason for this book. What is currently taking place in the marketing profession is a quiet revolution attracting little attention (not nearly so much, for example, as the glamour and exposure of advertising). At the epicenter of this quiet revolution is "human media," all the people involved in the marketing process. Motivating, training, and communicating with these people is a primary objective of nonmedia marketing.

The "people priority" character of today's marketing environment dramatizes the need for an entrepreneurial attitude. Our overwhelming purpose here, consequently, is to affirm that *promotion is an art, not a science.* What we hope to accomplish is to define the needs of that art. The reader will not be rewarded at the end with a convenient, tightly constructed formula for promoting a product or service. Because of this lack of formula, this absence of discernible pattern, he or she will not be able to take this art form and make a science out of it. Granted, the reader can be scientific with segments of it (much in the manner that the buying of media is more scientific than the creative aspects of advertising), but the more important aspects for the reader to understand are promotion's role and its evolving nature. With that kind of preparation, we hope the marketer will begin to attack the problems of the product, remembering that his work is *not* a science, but an art.

Bud Frankel
H. W. Phillips

Acknowledgments

Many, many thanks go to all those who helped in the composition of this book—all the folks at Frankel & Company who in anonymous roles contributed to the information about the sales promotion industry and promotion programs, past and present; *Advertising Age* as an on-going news source for the past several years and the columnists who have appeared there, lending their insights to what appears here, people such as Robert M. Prentice, Louis J. Haugh, and others; the *Sales Promotion Monitor;* Dr. Roger Strang and the Marketing Science Institute for important research; Peter Francese for his work in demographics; Imogene Gemberling for her work on transcriptions of interviews; and the marketing students at Purdue University, North Central Campus, whose opinions helped in the early drafts.

And, of course, to our wives, who stood it all.

Contents

Part I

Overview

CHAPTER 1

Increasing Importance of Promotion

Attesting to the increasing importance of promotion are the success stories in nonmedia marketing. One well-known company in the communications field reached 126 percent of its six-month goal in seven weeks. A packaged-goods manufacturer boosted sales of one of its products 600 percent in one month. And an insurance company reaped a million-dollar profit on a $95,000 investment.

Each of the successes was the result of a well-planned, well-executed sales promotion program. The first involved a sales motivation program; the second, a retail merchandising event; and the third, a direct response effort.

The *measurable effectiveness* of sales promotion—which these three examples demonstrate—is a major reason why promotion has grown at a faster rate than media advertising over the past 15 years. Today, consumer and trade promotions account for nearly 60 percent of the total marketing budgets of U.S. businesses.[1] Some estimate that nonmedia marketing expenditures will exceed $60 billion in 1985.[2]

Ours is a society in motion, and we are continuing to evolve in new directions. Ever-changing life styles, media clutter, rapid technological innovations, turbulent economic conditions, and dramatic demographic shifts are but a few factors that affect our lives. Decentralization in business, politics, and in culture is a growing trend; diversity is encouraged in every walk of life.[3] All these factors, as well as many others, are influencing buyer/seller relationships and therefore the way marketers reach their markets. Marketing management, consequently, is now recognizing the need for more efficient use of promotion budgets. As expenditures are viewed more closely and as the selling effort becomes an ever-more-costly proposition, marketers are turning to innovative tools that bring predictable results. The following are some specific reasons for the increased importance of promotion:

Management has become more receptive to promotion. The successful use of rebates by auto and appliance manufacturers, and of coupons by airlines, has reinforced the legitimacy of promotion as a marketing tool. After a recent United Airlines strike was settled, half-fare coupons helped United fill its seats again in one month instead of the expected nine months.

The growth of the product management system has encouraged increases in promotional spending. The pressure on product managers for quick results makes them look to sales promotion for the answers.

The increasing number of products in the marketplace has resulted in increased use of promotion to gain the attention and effort of the sales force, to encourage the trade to stock the product, and to persuade the consumer to try it. Competition is chipping away at the dominance of many companies.

Changing economic conditions—rising prices, material shortages, energy crises, skyrocketing costs of money—have caused manufacturers to use new and heavier promotion tactics. Inventory pressures, intensified by high interest rates, are compelling companies to seek new ways of gaining faster turnovers to keep inventories at minimum levels.

Increasing media costs—the average cost of a 30-second TV spot has increased 55 percent in the past three years—three times that of the inflation rate.[4] Magazine rates have increased 23 percent, newspaper rates 30 percent, and local radio rates 24 percent. Advertising budgets are not keeping up with these increased media costs, which means that companies are not getting the audiences they formerly reached.[5] Advertising production costs have continued to climb—$200,000 for a commercial production is no longer an exception.

Trade is putting increasing pressure on manufacturers because retailers are seeing their costs increase. The trade views allowances and deals as ways of boosting profits and therefore wants more of this financial help from manufacturers. The whole subject of deals and dealing has major implications all along the marketing-sales path. To the marketing manager, dealing is a way to increase his brand's volume or market share over that of the previous year. To the sales manager, dealing is a way to stimulate the sales force to meet the current month's quota. To salespeople, dealing is something that helps them convince the buyer to stock up. To buyers, dealing is the most important part of their jobs.

An equally important reason for the increase in promotion is *demographic trends.*[6] However marketers measure the cause and effect relationships that are changing the market, they know that the United States is being transformed by unprecedented demographic changes. And these trends will continue to have profound influence on any organization marketing consumer products or services.

We are directly concerned with three aspects of population change:

1. Changing age structure and how it influences consumer behavior.

2. Household trends.
3. Complex regional population shifts.[7]

DEMOGRAPHICS: CHANGING AGE STRUCTURE

By 1990 about 21 million people will be added to the population by birth and immigration. Though legal in-migration has been controlled at about 400,000 annually, undocumented immigration, especially from Latin America, is growing. The annual net illegal immigration is about half a million. These new arrivals, who are for the most part Spanish-speaking, are revitalizing major cities such as New York, Los Angeles, and Miami. Currently, Hispanics are the fastest-growing minority group in the United States.

Although births in the 1970s declined to about 3 million per year (from 4 million in the 50s and 60s), that number will rise again in the 1980s primarily because more women will be in the child-bearing age range.

The teenage population is declining. This is bad news for companies marketing such products as stereos and shampoo. The good news is that a significantly higher proportion of teenagers have jobs. The number of young adults in their early 20s is also declining, as is the marriage rate for women in this group: where only about one third of women 20 to 24 had never married in 1970, nearly half are unmarried today. Most men and women in this age group are not living with their parents but are in the labor force. They therefore pose special problems for promotional efforts.

People in their 30s and 40s are rapidly growing in number. Representing one fourth of the entire population (over 40 million people are expected to be in their 30s by 1990, nearly double the figure for 1970), they will dominate the market for consumer goods and services in the coming decade. By 1990 those in their 40s will be the most rapidly growing age group. People in their 40s are generally more affluent and more stable than those in younger age groups. According to William Cox, an economist with the Department of Commerce, as the population ages and becomes more affluent, there will be a trend away from mass-produced goods toward individualized goods and services.

More than 12 million women will enter the labor force in

the next 10 years in addition to the unprecedented number of women now working. By 1990, two thirds of all women 18 to 64 will be in the labor force, representing many empty homes in the daytime. Any product or service that will save time for the working woman, and is promoted that way, will do very well. The sale of microwave ovens today illustrates this fact.

HOUSEHOLD TRENDS

The average household size is declining, and families with more than three children are becoming rare. More than half of all households now consist of one or two persons, so telephone answering devices, for example, are selling well because there is rarely anyone home to answer the telephone. Type of household is also changing. Nonfamilies, persons living alone or with other nonrelated people, now represent almost one third of all households.

Married-couple families are declining as a percent of total households. The stereotypical concept of the American family—married-couple families where dad works and mom stays home—now represents only 28 percent of all American households. The only household type to decline from 1970 to 1980 is married-couple families with children. This decline has occurred despite a 25 percent growth in total households. The fastest-growing household type is that of the single woman with one or more children. Nearly 80 percent of these household heads are in the labor force.

The population 65 years old and over is growing at over twice the rate of the total population. The population 75 and older is growing even faster. Since 1974, life expectancy has risen substantially faster than in the previous decade. The average person born today can expect to live 75 years (men 71, women 78), four years more than in 1970.

The demand for nursing home beds, other medical care facilities, and social services for the elderly will continue to grow well into the next century.

COMPLEX REGIONAL POPULATION SHIFTS

Migration trends within the United States are very complex, but their net effect is a continuing decline in central city population. Suburban areas are still growing, but rural areas are growing equally as fast. Smaller communities outside metropolitan centers are attracting industry and people who are willing to forgo urban opportunities for the benefits of small-town life. For the first time, the majority of our population lives in the South and West—Northeast and North Central regions have experienced substantial out-migration. This pattern may continue but at a slower rate. The Northeast is the first part of the United States to achieve zero population growth (often referred to as ZPG); and New York state leads in out-migration with a net loss of over half a million people since 1970.

There are two major problems with ZPG: (1) $50 billion per year is transferred from the federal government to state and local governments based largely on population. Revenue sharing is a good example. Generally, when the population declines, the amount of money transferred declines. (2) The Northeast and North Central regions of the United States have large fixed costs in urban infrastructures and need to know how to manage with less federal help.

Such changes in demographic trends affect everything that is promoted and sold. Hence, when a company is planning a promotion, it must think about which demographic group it wishes to target and then learn as much as possible about *where* and *how* these people live. Regionality as related to promotion must be defined in terms of lifestyle differences and regional preferences for certain products, package styles, flavors, and sizes. Regional preferences indeed dictate marketing practices; and people in sales and marketing must respond accordingly.

CHAPTER 2

Recent History of the Promotion Business, 1950–1980

Modern society has always engaged in activities to promote the sale of some product or idea. Even in matters of personal salesmanship, Shakespeare, for one, advised: "For I must tell you friendly in your ear,/ Sell what you can. You are not for all markets" (*As You Like It*, III, v, 59–60).

Toward the end of the last century (1895), John H. Patterson, founder of the National Cash Register Company, conceived what might have been the earliest indirect sales promotion idea for his existing customers. He thought that "if he could in some way help these merchants to become more successful they would soon need more and better cash registers to handle their increased business."[1]

Early in the 20th century, Richard Sears in *The Sears, Roebuck & Co. Catalog* of 1908 (the 18th edition of what A. C. Roebuck started in 1891) "became one of the first merchandisers to utilize effectively the 'loss leader.' In the last eight pages of the catalog the potential customer finds two-page spreads displaying all sorts of small items...priced at 2¢, 4¢, 6¢, or 8¢ each. ... This promotion had a twofold purpose: First, it encouraged the cautious to 'gamble' and find out how easy it really was to place a mail order with Sears; and second, it started people writing orders to which they would then add higher-priced merchandise from other parts of the book."[2] And at that time the Sears catalog had even more surprises for its readers.

Ever since then, products, in one way or another, have been advertised and promoted with the needs and wants of consumers in mind. Early signs of today's marketplace conditions appeared after World War II, and that is where the modern sales promotion story really begins. To know its beginnings is to understand its preeminence in the 1980s.

THE FIRST POSTWAR DECADE— THE "SHOW" YEARS, THE 1950s

In the early days of sales promotion the public believed *everything* that promoted or advertised a product or service emanated from an "advertising agency." This belief endured, even though advertising agencies primarily handled media, and it is strongly held even today. The sales promotion organizations and the sales promotion writers were aware of this misinformed view. They went on working, however, and soon found themselves in a kind of limbo. They were the early solution seekers and ghost writers for the problems of distribution.

The 1950s was the decade of production, prosperity, and industrial growth. These relatively easy years for marketers were characterized by the tremendous pent-up demand unleashed after World War II. Production was readily absorbed by demand, and at times product was in short supply. Manufacturers of consumer goods (e.g., food, major and traffic appliances, laundry products, hardware, cosmetics) had a simple strategy—produce great numbers of displays to show the product and distribute elaborate literature about the product. If they showed their products at all, they sold them. The "Show" years, in fact, reached well into the 1960s.

The promotion agency business then consisted largely of graphic services provided by art studios or display houses. Agencies and studios tended to be reactive rather than proactive, providing only those services and materials that the client requested, from simple product copy to complex art and imaginative animated displays.

What emerged from this economic phenomenon was a new breed of entrepreneurs—the sales promotion agency. The agency was usually a small shop that provided outstanding design work. In fact, design skills made it possible for the "agency" to function as a broker in the production of graphics and manufactured materials needed to support the design. This brokerage function became the principal source of income and profit for the agency of the "Show" decade.

A popular misconception then, as now, was that these materials were forms of advertising and were therefore created by an advertising agency. Yet advertising agencies, particularly larger ones, resisted clients' requests for help unless the problem directly related to media advertising. This reluctance further stimulated the growth of the promotion agency. While many of these shops began to enjoy long-term working relationships with their clients, it was a rare occurrence for any promotion agency to work under a contract. Almost all assignments were handled on an individual project basis and were not significantly related to what preceded them or what might follow.

THE SECOND POSTWAR DECADE— THE "TELL" YEARS, THE 1960s

While many sales promotion agencies grew in importance from their inception in the 1950s to the early 1960s, recognition of sales promotion's potential was still a few years away. We now see in retrospect that the 1960s became the decade of advertising. If a manufacturer could *tell* about his product, forcefully enough and often enough, he could move merchandise.

This was the decade when the Alberto-Culver Company, as an innovator, designated 55 percent of its revenue for advertising and changed for all time the ratio of advertising-to-sales on health and beauty aids. This was the decade when leading advertisers everywhere in the United States began placing an extraordinary amount of advertising weight behind packaged goods products.

The creative advertising boutique first made its appearance during the "Tell" decade. Creative advertising for Benson and Hedges cigarettes exploited the alleged difficulties caused by the extra length of a 100-millimeter cigarette. Alka Seltzer used some zany lifestyle situations to call attention to new and expanded uses of the product. At the same time, TV was maturing as a communications and information medium. Audiences were flocking to the tube, making it the most efficient (and only mass) medium available.

Despite excellent beginnings and momentary triumphs, sales promotion agencies, because they were small and because of the nature of their income, found it exceedingly difficult to hang on. To advertising agencies and many others, promotion was an afterthought. It was a pariah of the industry, the brother-in-law on the living room sofa. In many cases, promotion as a program did not even exist. It was a thing, or groups of things.

Promotion was called *collateral.* Where the term came from as applied to sales promotion is hard to determine, and there is the allegation, difficult to take seriously, that *collateral* was the invention of media people who disdainfully relegated sales promotion to a "garbage can" status of creativity. The more visionary sales promotion specialists—to whom the very utterance of the word was repugnant—felt that promotion was collateral, in fact, to nothing. They admitted, however, that promotion was then used precisely as collateral. It was an ingredient that could be done without most of the time. All one had to do was *tell* people about the product.

The fact that many sales promotion agencies gravitated to where the action was reinforced the notion that sales promotion agencies were indeed producers of "things." They moved toward their strengths, to what was best for them. What was best for most, of course, was the kind of business that produced the highest volume of dollars. Naturally, the highest dollar volume areas were displays and display packages. Movement to displays was a decision that had to be made. One could only make payroll and pay the rent with volume business, which display and display-package orders represented. "Interesting" promotions and "exciting" promotional ideas without volume production of materials going into the marketplace were the romantic sides of the business. Such aspects, however, meant little in the struggle to stay solvent. Retrenching, for some, was the order of the day; and it was a challenge to have implicit faith in the rightness of sales promotion's future. Some had that faith, some did not. Those who did not were satisfied with being recognized as producers of *things* so long as they sold promotional programs tied closely to the display aspect of the business. For the time being, what did it matter?

Things indeed preceded ideas; the process bore a reverse logic: "Hey! Somebody think up a good headline for this display!"

Evolution demands patience from its witnesses. The faithful realized that promotion sorely needed a discipline which, at that point, it lacked. That sales promotion lacked such discipline is of little wonder since many promotions were developed by production-oriented people, art studio sales representatives, printing house personnel, and art buyers. They worked on the basis of creating promotions that would somehow reach enough right people to motivate them to action, unmindful that they might also reach too many wrong people. They were concerned with *how* they could produce a promotion, not *why* they should do it. Too many promotions lacked a supportive idea to answer the question, "Why?"

Inevitably, however, the promotion people selling or creating the idea were not sufficiently involved with the client company to answer the *why* question in anything but superficial terms.

In the decade of the 1960s, marketing management began asking, "Is there something that we can add to what we're currently doing to make us more effective?" As an answer to this question, the first signs of promotion's marketing implications began to appear. What was the *idea?* What are you going to do differently? How are you going to approach this *particular* audience?

THE DECADE OF THE 1970s— OVERTURE TO THE 1980s

When we view the past dozen years as a single calendar of events, seeing them as a tableau of change and comparing them with the previous 15 years, the startling difference between the decades of the 1970s and the 1960s becomes apparent. Sales promotion's gain in importance (and prestige) was a gain for all of marketing.

Because marketing became much broader and much more complex than it had been in the production and advertising decades, marketing management began to look more closely at all of its different publics and audiences (sales force, distribution, and retailer, as well as consumer). Managers saw that individual publics had changing needs. The more aggressive, more watchful sales promotion agency changed accordingly, and an audience-based "need recognition" developed within its ranks.

These ingredients—"need" and "need recognition"—became indispensable to a new kind of partnership—promotion and marketing. And several developments brightened the futures for both partners.

First, the complexion of the sales promotion agency changed: sales representatives became account executives. To outsiders such a change may seem superficial, but along with the title came a change in function. Sales representatives, given the nature of the sales promotion agency's income, tended to tout what they sold, fabricating sales stories to rationalize why clients should buy from them. It was, and still is, a natural human tendency and an understandable one. Also understandable is the reluctance of clients to have "partnerships" with people who are always trying to sell them something when their "need" for advice and involvement is greater than ever before.

Establishment of the customer-client relationship was the function that defined the position and provided the prestige for the advertising agency account executive. With the new "partnership" between sales promotion agency account executives and their clients it was no longer necessary for promotion executives to pressure their clients into buying.

Second, the issue of exclusivity had to be resolved. Since promotion, this new "partner," began to make important contributions to sales goals and sales plans, it was now getting information that it could not get before. If the clients had an agency account executive servicing their business, they no longer wanted the agency servicing people in comparable or competitive industries.

Third, sales promotion's growing importance to marketing motivated management to want promotional organizations to be more involved in what was happening internally; and this could only occur with a long-term relationship, particularly a *contractual* relationship, to make promotion a "team" member in the clients' selling plans.

Fourth, with the sales promotion agency assuming a counselor role, methods of remuneration soon changed. In place of the old method of commissions came revenue on a fee basis for the hours worked and the professional staff used.

Management's commitment to the promotion discipline became a reality in the 1970s. It is interesting to learn the story from the client's side. By 1974, according to Russell D. Bowman, then Corporate Promotion Development Manager, General Foods Corporation, sales promotion's role had changed so dramatically that "sales promotion/merchandising has generally gained a status equal to other marketing functions."[3] From statistics he gathered, he pointed out that since 1969 sales promotion had (1) exceeded advertising expenditures in percentage of growth every year and (2) actually become larger than advertising in overall expenditures. Based on an average rate per year over those preceding six years, he projected promotion expenditures in 1974 to be $27.9 billion and those of advertising to be $19.4 billion during the same period, or 30 percent less.[4]

Mr. Bowman said further, "An overall look at the trends shows more use of media (to advertise promotions), which is why the sales promotion department is now involved with agencies and with media decisions."

To highlight the ever-growing importance of promotion, Mr. Bowman added:

> The effect of the nation's economic problems will not only change consumer attitudes and spending, but also the approach to marketing budgets. Management will look for more efficiency, less waste, and greater use of marketing that can communicate better *savings and value.*
>
> Traditionally, consumer promotions have been the most tangible method of accomplishing this end. However, with increased spending on promotion, management will look to even greater promotion expertise and experienced professionals to assure tighter budgeting and estimating.

> To respond to this dramatic condition...a series of sug-
> gestions for better marketing management include advertis-
> ing and promotion programs that pull together in a synergis-
> tic effect primarily as a result jointed marketing efforts in
> an atmosphere of crowded media and ever-increasing costs
> are considerable. Promotion will work into advertising pri-
> marily (but *not limited to*) magazines, supplements, and
> newspapers in order to have the investment in space serve a
> dual function. Additionally, many brands have clearly dem-
> onstrated that promotion...can contribute strongly to the
> development of a unique brand personality.
>   The future will see a more professional approach to adver-
> tising, promotion, and market research specialists working
> together.[5]

Equally significant in that period, the mid-1970s, was the
admission on the part of the nation's largest advertising
agencies that they had been acquiring an "overwhelming responsibility for a wide range of sales promotion activities for
their clients."[6] This admission was the result of a study conducted by the sales promotion committee of the American Association of Advertising Agencies and reviewed in an *Advertising Age* article by Louis J. Haugh on July 8, 1974. A detailed questionnaire was sent to 386 members, 55 percent of
whom answered—evidence alone of the accelerated interest
in sales promotion matters.

> The committee decided to study "sales promotion" practices
> and not "collateral," which has been the traditional agency
> approach to this part of the business. Among promotion peo-
> ple, collateral has the same negative connotation that "junk
> mail" has to direct mailers.
>   The study found that 100 percent of the respondents said
> they were involved in promotion planning for their clients,
> 96 percent were involved in promotion strategy, and 70 per-
> cent indicated involvement in promotion research.
>
>   *   *   *   *   *
>
> [T]he top 10 advertising agencies have been noticeably ac-
> tive in the sales promotion area in the last year.
>   The biggest, J. Walter Thompson Co., last April an-
> nounced it was upgrading its 11-year-old sales promotion de-
> partment to division status.

*   *   *   *   *

Last year [1973], of the 66 ad agencies billing more than $25 million [each], one third reported sales promotion billings averaging 8.8 percent of their total business. These 22 agencies did a total of $183,700,000 in promotional billings.

By comparison, of the top 56 agencies in 1968 with more than $25 million [each] in billings, 25 reported promotion billings averaging 4.5 percent of their billings total, or $117,300,000.

*   *   *   *   *

Among smaller agencies the sale of sales promotion is less clear, but the general assumption is that work on such things as sales sheets, direct mail, displays, meetings, trade shows, and other trade promotions accounts for a larger part of their business than such services do with the larger ad agencies. . . . *Those agencies that charge clients a fee appear to be more advantageously positioned to handle sales promotion work for clients* [italics added].

If ad agencies are taking a fresh look at promotion work for clients, who has been providing this work for advertisers up until now? The great bulk of the business, estimated at $18 billion per year, is done in-house by clients who deal directly with suppliers of such things as premiums or P.O.P.

There also are a number of agencies which specialize in sales promotion services. [A spokesman] said that he expects growing competition from ad agencies. "However, as a rule of thumb, ad agencies don't know how to produce and sell sales promotion at a profit," he said.[7]

There were many other voices that recognized the symptoms of change. In his talk at the *Advertising Age* Creative Workshop in the summer of 1974, Tom Dillon, then-president of Batten, Barton, Durstine & Osborn Advertising Agency, touched on the problem of much-needed promotion. He spoke of advertising as a one-way communication that attempts to affect human decision. Although advertising frequently depends on human memory, its message "content is attenuated before the reader makes a decision."[8] That same year, Paul Harper, Chairman of the Board of Needham, Harper, and Steers Advertising Agency, characterized the agency of the future and stressed that it would have a much broader range

of services than it does presently with high emphasis on promotion. One need not have looked further, in fact, than the
Dartnell Sales Promotion Handbook for recognition of sales
promotion's accelerating importance. The editors of the sixth
edition (1973), summarizing the consensus of its marketing
contributors, reported the following (primarily for the benefit
of management executives):

> ...marketing and its essential ingredient, sales promotion,
> will play an ever-increasingly important role on the eco-
> nomic stage of the country in the next 10 years.
>
> As an integral part of marketing, advertising and sales
> promotion executives should never lose sight of the fact that
> their functions have very definite relationships with corpo-
> rate marketing goals and with long-term marketing policies,
> as well as immediate sales objectives.
>
> From the standpoint of personal advancement, the sales
> promotion executive who displays genuine interest in, and
> demonstrates an appreciation of, his company's broad mar-
> keting problems will advance more rapidly up the corporate
> ladder.[9]

Before the end of the decade, projections of sales promotion
expenditures reached $30 billion; and by 1981, evidence
seemed to indicate that that figure had risen to $50 billion.
There is, nevertheless, a curious and ironic side to these ac-
knowledgments. Though gathering figures by *types* of sales
promotion activities (from the display industry, the trade
show industry, etc.) seemed statistically feasible, the advertisers and their advertising agencies, those who had actually
spent the money, had not traditionally broken down their
billings by sources to corroborate the findings.[10]

It is not surprising, then, that marketing management,
very generally, was incredulous. "Now, wait a minute! If
we're spending all that money, where did it go? Promotion is
getting very important, and we must make certain that we're
putting the right kinds of people in charge of auditing and
creating what we need."

A July-August 1976 article in the *Harvard Business Review*
("Sales Promotion—Fast Growth, Faulty Management," by
Roger A. Strang, then professor of marketing at the University of Southern California) put this problem in the proper
perspective.

The Strang Report[11]

In conducting a study for the Marketing Science Institute, Strang interviewed "54 executives from 17 leading American consumer goods manufacturers and advertising agencies."[12] He made careful use of statistical data already available in formulating a report that stressed (1) the already existing prominence of sales promotion as a marketing activity and (2) the already existing preeminence of sales promotion over advertising in total expenditures. These facts were already established, but his corroboration had the blessing of the American Association of Advertising Agencies whose Educational Foundation provided the funding for Strang's research.

Strang's contentions provided the following insights for many companies that apparently were not aware of the true nature of their own spending.

1. Many companies and their advertising agencies did not know, and have not known, how much they spent on sales promotion activities. To begin with, a good estimate of how much is spent on sales promotion activities had never been compiled. Even though the definitions of *advertising* and *promotion* compound the difficulties of compilation, Strang's review of existing data revealed that some major promotion elements were more important than advertising and they were increasing rapidly.

    . . . promotion spending increased twice as fast as that of advertising between 1969 and 1975. Assuming this trend continues, 1976 expenditures on these selected promotion activities will total over $30 billion compared with just $20.5 billion for regular media advertising. . . . From these data it appears that between 1968 and 1975 the proportion of total advertising and promotion spending devoted to promotion increased from 53 percent to 59 percent. Other studies have supported this trend and found it to be even more marked in certain categories. The market for consumer nondurables is one example. And among manufacturers selling these types of products to grocery stores, the proportion of advertising and promotion budgets allocated to promotion increased from 54 percent in 1968 to 65 percent in 1972. . . . Moreover, the growth in promotion spending is not simply a matter of increased expenditures by promotion-oriented companies, but rather of more widespread use of sales promotion techniques.

* * * * *

They [expenditure figures] indicate a major change in the importance of a generally neglected area of marketing strategy.

This change may pass unnoticed in many companies because of a failure to record promotion expenditures separately. In some companies these expenditures are included with advertising; in others they may be considered as part of the sales force's expenses or perhaps go in a general marketing account. Even when companies do have separate promotion accounts, they may not record *all* promotion charges. For example, the extra product required for a bonus pack may be recorded as a manufacturing expense, or the cost of special labels or packs charged to packaging. The loss of revenue from a temporary price reduction may not be recorded at all.[13]

2. Those same companies did not know, and have not known, what returns they have gotten on their investments. Strang includes this fact, a corollary to No. 1, because increased expenditures on promotion is not a virtue in itself. Because of the overall neglect of where the money is going specifically, and partly because of lax accounting procedures, in many organizations, no one knows the kind of return being accrued for this substantial investment. "In one market for a frequently purchased consumer product, the advertising/promotion mix of the three leading brands reversed from 63/37 in 1969 to 22/79 in 1972."[14] The consequent return on such an investment switch, Strang suggests, is probably unknown.

3. There have been very specific reasons internally why and how promotion activities have increased so dramatically: First, *"promotion has become more acceptable.* Several executives reported an increased willingness by senior management to view promotion as an acceptable marketing activity." The executives are apparently increasingly interested in promotion because they have forsaken the notion that promotion "cheapened" a brand; they have gained a new respect for its successes. One example of a promotion success involves ". . . the use of rebates by auto and appliance manufacturers in 1974 and 1975."[15]

Second, *"more executives are better qualified.* The appointment of more executives with better qualifications to positions of responsibility for promotion has also helped growth."[16] For example, the "established position of sales promotion manager has been upgraded from supervision of point-of-purchase production or premium purchases to activity involving broad responsibility for promotion planning."[17]

Third, *"the product manager looks for quick returns...* the widespread adoption of the product manager system has also encouraged increases in promotion spending. This system frequently requires prompt demonstration of results for fast progress up the corporate ladder; promotion programs are usually implemented more quickly and produce results sooner than advertising."[18]

4. There have been very specific reasons externally (i.e., in the business environment) why the change in sentiments about promotion has occurred. The most important of these is that since brands have increased so rapidly in number, and since their introduction relies so heavily on promotion, expenditures for the promotion function have also increased. "This proliferation of brands makes the use of promotion more likely as companies seek their share of the *limited retail shelf space"* [italics added].[19] Second, competitors are realizing the advantages of using sales promotion, and as a result they are becoming more promotion-minded. "The adoption of an aggressive strategy by one brand in 1970 led to a 450 percent increase in promotion expenditures by the three major competing brands in its market in three years."[20] Third, trade pressure has grown. "The increased size and sophistication of chain supermarkets, drugstores, discount houses, and other retailers has [sic] brought increased pressure on manufacturers for support and allowances."[21]

5. Management seems in many instances to be ineffective in understanding the determination of its own expenditures, and there are specific indications why this is so. Strang's survey revealed, surprisingly, that promotion programs rarely have established objectives and "when they are established, are not likely to be in quantitative terms."[22] This seemed to be true, he learned, in both overall plans and in individual programs.

The budgeting procedures seem especially indicative of management's ineffectiveness because they are not likely to involve "extensive consideration of cost effectiveness.... The usual approach may be: 'How much did we have to spend last year? How much have we got to spend this year? How will we cut it up?'"[23]

Strang observed that management commonly allocated a percentage of anticipated sales to promotions. This allocation method might work except that the decision to do so has been frequently a cart-before-the-horse one. The amount allocated often "depends more on corporate financial requirements than on marketing strategy. This amount may be related to advertising in some arbitrary way, perhaps by a desire to keep a fixed ratio of advertising to promotion. Another method has been the leftover approach "...a fixed percentage of sales is allocated to both advertising and promotion, with promotion getting what is left after advertising has been budgeted."[24]

This further observation is noteworthy. Several studies "...demonstrated that advertising and promotion interact 'synergistically' to produce higher sales than an equivalent investment in *either alone*. Yet in many companies the advertising and promotion budgets are prepared independently" [italics added].[25]

6. There are several ways in which promotion management can improve its effectiveness. In support of this contention, Strang recommended that management analyze spending, establish objectives, select appropriate promotion and pretest techniques, and evaluate promotions in depth.[26]

By 1976, the mere act of allocating funds to both advertising and promotion was no longer satisfactory; the *way* they were apportioned had a significant effect on brand sales and brand profits. The strategy of allocating advertising and promotion funds separately was not a new one. It was a conclusion made public (the same year as the Strang Report) after a 10-year marketing study of two major brands of grocery store products conducted by marketing consultant Robert M. Prentice and the Marketing Science Institute.[27]

"...at the end of 10 years, these two brands that were so nearly equal during the earlier years were not even in the same league. Brand A's annual sales in year 10 were up 94 percent over year 1, but Brand B's were down 12 percent. More importantly, Brand A's annual profit had increased by 120 percent, while Brand B's had fallen a disastrous 40 percent."[28]

According to Prentice, "the major reason for these differences lies in the way these two brands apportioned their marketing funds between advertising and *certain types* of promotion." By using what he calls the "Consumer Franchise Building" approach (CFB), a marketing-management analysis relating "brand expenditures on advertising and promotion to sales and market share," Prentice contended that "the real need was to consider what goes on in the consumer's mind and [to determine] how each type of marketing activity works to build long-term brand preference and to influence short-term decisions to buy." (For a detailed discussion of CFB versus Non-CFB activities from the study, see pages 49–51.)

Especially significant in the study was Prentice's observation that although "advocates of heavier promotion appear to be winning the argument against advertising agencies that push media advertising," and "promotion expenditures now represent an estimated 60 percent of total marketing expenditures, ... this growing promotion emphasis often is based on short-term considerations, assumptions, and personal opinion—some of doubtful validity."[29]

In speaking of his work with the Marketing Science Institute on the study of the advertising/promotion mix, Prentice further observed that the study was one "that identifies serious weaknesses in the way that many package goods companies plan their promotions and incorporate them into their marketing programs."[30]

Strang and Prentice were not the only ones who suggested greater awareness, and pointed out pitfalls, to the distribution of the total marketing budget. In 1979, the Donnelley Company conducted a survey of 50 major packaged goods companies, and its survey "indicated the average split of the total marketing budget was 40.5 percent for advertising and 59.5 percent for promotion."[31]

In March 1981, Fred L. Lemont of the Lemont Consulting Group, New York, citing the Donnelley survey as well as his own, also observed the general management neglect of promotion analysis. Though his particular purpose was largely to illustrate the vast opportunity available to marketing management, his own analysis concerns us here.[32] Lemont contends essentially that major companies (he sampled 40) have consistently spent large sums of money with their advertising agencies for the content and management of their advertising dollar and for "various forms of measurement and analysis of advertising effectiveness." In addition, the companies maintain "large in-house advertising management groups," despite that their systems "for tracking trade and consumer promotion effectiveness" are virtually nonexistent. If they exist at all, they are insignificant in number. By the questions he asks subsequently, he implies that there is very little "pretesting or in-market testing of trade or consumer promotion" and very little knowledge of the "long-term effect of trade promotion on brand profits."[33]

Hammering a few more nails in this coffin of neglect, Lemont cites the following factors as some reasons for the insufficient efforts at sales promotion control.

> In the past 15 years promotion has grown in absolute terms faster than media advertising. Yet, it is still managed much the way it was when it was 5 percent of the marketing budget rather than its current 60 percent. Promotion management techniques have not grown with budgets in the 1970s as advertising management techniques did in the 1960s.
>
> Some companies consider trade promotion a price discount rather than a marketing expense. If it is not an expense, it literally does not exist and, therefore, does not have to be managed.
>
> Trade promotion is frequently perceived as inevitable—driven by competitive action, trade and industry practice and, therefore, uncontrollable.
>
> Some companies do believe they are measuring trade promotion. The best of these measurements, computerized or noncomputerized, detail sales results, promotion period vs. base period. Basically, measurements show [that] you sell more on deal than not on deal. This is sales reporting, not sales analysis.

The dependence of many companies (not sales departments, but companies) on trade promotion to make volume goals is growing. And it is true many companies do not want to recognize how dependent they are.[34]

To anyone familiar with marketing studies made in the last 10 years, there can be little question that sales promotion has become the essential and dominating ingredient in the marketing mix. By the end of the 1970s, those who had been heeding the signs recognized the importance of promotion.

THE DECADE OF THE 1980s— THE COMING OF AGE

The principal influences of what happened in the 1970s did not begin to surface in the marketplace until the 1980s. Compounded by severely changing economic conditions, increasing media costs, and the growth of the product management system, sales promotion has increased in importance as a marketing fact of life. No longer an afterthought, no longer an activity exclusive of other marketing alternatives, sales promotion, or nonmedia marketing, is preeminent over media as a marketing tool, attested to by the vast expenditures devoted to it, its measurable effectiveness in its success stories, and its acceptability by marketing management.

Sales promotion's acceptance by marketing management cannot be overestimated. Not only has management given full recognition to promotional techniques employed to distribute and sell its products, but it has also recognized the viability of the sales promotion agency, which frequently functions as an equal partner with the advertising agency in planning successful strategies to distribute and sell the client's products.

Sales professionals today tell us that so many changes have occurred in the marketplace in the last three to five years—not from the top down, but from the bottom up, beginning with consumer preferences—that they are now on the threshold of solving many new problems.

A well-recognized current problem is the presence of product and service *parity*. Product and service innovations are becoming less a factor in the purchase decision. In today's marketing environment, products and services are becoming so similar that additional inducements are often required. A good example is illustrated by the homogeneous service offered in the airline industry. To the consumer, the only real difference between airlines is the name of each airline. Their services, equipment, and flight schedules are all similar, and since the consumer is often aware of the route structures and names of the companies as well as the services they offer, marketing strategies to attract new customers must be implemented by additional (and to date unused) marketing tools.

The retail grocery business is another example of the parity problem. Marketing power in the United States is shifting rapidly from the *brand* itself to the retailer who is talking to people, sensing change, keeping pace, and performing the art of promotion. Evidence of the reduced importance of the brand name is overwhelming. The growth of the generic product, the no-label product; the growth of private-label products; the growth of warehouse stores and box stores where the consumer is invited to save money, all illustrate brand names' diminishing power to market products.

That frequently used term *marketing mix* has become extremely important in attacking the problems faced by the marketing profession. In every case a "mix" of marketing strategies appropriate to new problem-solving demands creative ideas that take into account the new, more confident consumer who can relegate products and services to parity status. New ideas surface infrequently, particularly when everyone in marketing is reading the same research material and drawing the same conclusions. If the process were easy, all programs would succeed; but all programs do not succeed. We are, moreover, still in a period where various marketing services consider themselves each more important than the others and will attempt to sell all comers, even for self-preservation, an understandable tactic but not in the interests of their customers.

Today there is a new task for sales promotion professionals. They can no longer rely on their "favorite" promotion tactic to solve every problem. They must understand the *needs* of every step in the distribution chain. They must develop the appropriate strategies to satisfy those needs. Finally, they must mix the many available promotional tactics into a *unique selling program* tailored to the category, the brand, the distribution, and the consumer.

The future will belong to those marketing professionals and promotion agencies that recognize the complexity of the task and that invest the necessary energy to develop the ideas that permit successful escape from the parity trap.

CHAPTER 3

Definitions and Concepts

There is an old, often-told anecdote about a man whose house suffered substantial damage from a tornado. In great distress, he telephoned his architect and exclaimed, "You'll have to come down here right away. We had a terrible tornado last night, and the architecture blew off my house!" To him, the relationship between architecture and his dwelling was never clear; architecture was simply something added on.

An understanding of sales promotion and its inseparable relationship to marketplace activities imposes similar demands on the promotion professional. First of all, the professional must understand the *environment* of sales promotion. Only then is a definition understandable, but that definition must also be conceptually clear, accurate, and complete.

THE MARKETING TRIANGLE[1]

The traditional marketing approach from the manufacturer to the consumer is some form of controllable advertising; it can be depicted graphically as one side of a triangle. Whatever form the advertising takes—electronic media (television or radio), print media (magazines or newspapers), billboards, car cards, etc.—the marketer is generally able to control what he employs. He hires an advertising agency to fulfill tasks that involve research, creativity, and media placement. When the actual advertisement is placed, the marketer is reasonably assured that it will run at a specific time and expose a specific audience to its message. In that sense, advertising in its various forms is delivered via controlled media. Networks have even developed "make goods," a method they use to "make good" for any shortfall from anticipated audience delivery.

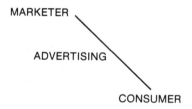

Sales promotion activity is much the opposite; there are no controls. It deals in human media, and there is no way to ensure that the intended message reaches its audience exactly as it was created. Sales promotion involves the human aspect and encourages people to behave in a predictable manner—*to behave in terms of each individually planned program.*

A manufacturer must take the products or services from the factory through the channels of distribution without the benefit of absolute control over the communication. These channels of distribution are extremely important because consumers have many different products and services to choose from.

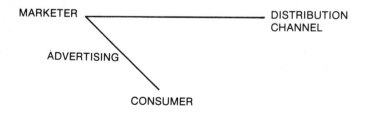

The manufacturer (now marketer) consequently has to contend with a great deal of parity in the marketplace. All the activities necessary to move the product to and through the channels of distribution to reach the consumer must be successful if the manufacturer is to make a sale.

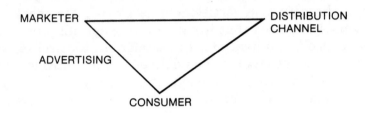

The product then goes to the sales force. The sales force must be armed with the appropriate tools and programs to motivate the distributor to stock, finance, promote, and sell the product through his sales force. The distributor's salespeople must, in turn, motivate the retailer, through tools and programs provided by the distributor, to stock, promote, feature, and actively sell the product to the consumer.

In developing programs to sell the manufacturer's product, today's sales promotion professional approaches the problem by offering *marketing services,* a new concept embracing sales promotion, to move a product through the channels of distribution successfully. *Marketing services* are consequently concerned with all the tasks in those distribution channels. The marketing services agency, the sales promotion professional's organization (see Part IV, Chapter 23), communicates with and motivates all those involved, including, ultimately, the consumer.

In terms of the diagram, then, the *marketing triangle* becomes a *marketing communication chain* for all who participate in the product's distribution.

Although the tasks are numerous and complex, at each point along the triangle (i.e., the chain of distribution), the process consists of two basic components: (1) creation and development of programs and (2) communication. Throughout, the process becomes communication, receptivity, communication, receptivity, communication, receptivity. This process influences many people all along the distribution line. All actions are interrelated.

Let's assume that a promotion has been developed. The client's promotion manager must communicate to sales management what that promotion activity will be. The sales manager is now a receiver, and the promotion department wants him to accept and support the promotion enthusiastically because he is the person who must now go out and sell it.

The sales manager must first call in his regional salespeople. He has to say to them, "Here is the idea we are going with, and this is the idea we're going to use to achieve our sales objectives." He is now a communicator, and he will communicate with the regional salespeople on much the same basis that the marketing people have communicated with him. He will have gone through the rationale, all the reasons why, and all the potential implications; and his own sales management will have coordinated plans with the shipping, packaging, operations, financial, and legal departments. The whole promotion will have been put together in a very thoughtful way.

Each of the regional sales managers must now go out and train and communicate to his sales forces what this promotion (selling) idea is, how it is used, what its implications are for them, and how it will alter (possibly) their professional thought processes. They may be required, after all, to do something different from what they have ever done before.

As communicators now, the regional salespeople will each call on their distributor principals. Each will say to the distributor, ". . . you are a world-famous television [for example] distributor, and we've got a new program for you. We've got this advertising and we've got that promotion, and you are going to love the way they work together to make your selling job easier."

And the distributor will say, "It looks pretty good but it's a back-breaker. We've never done anything like this before. How am I going to communicate this to my sales force?"

The distributor is then told that the promotion includes a whole new set of selling tools to be used by the sales force. Further, the distributor is told, "We are going to introduce a new product. . . we're going into the stereo business."

"We've never been in the stereo business before. . . . "

"We are going to introduce the stereo with a package of records. . . . "

"But we've never handled records before."

"...and we are going to pack them with your opening order along with point-of-sale material."

"How do I go about finding space in a retail store with this new brand? This big point-of-sale piece that you've got...I mean, that's absurd. There isn't any room on the retailer's floor the way it is, and none of those big brains in the corporate world has any thoughts about that."

"Well, yes, we have. We've researched a number of the retailers and created a display that fits over the product and hangs from the ceiling. And there will be an array of sales promotion tools for each of your retailers."

And so forth. By anticipating the objections, the marketer has provided all the selling tools for each step through the distribution channel to the bottom of the triangle. In a successful, properly conceived promotion, the marketer will make each one of the receivers a communicator and will equip them with the proper tools to motivate the next person in distribution.

From a directional viewpoint, then, the pattern through the channels of distribution, after a promotional program has been developed, after the need for involvement is satisfied (see Chapter 5, Promotion: Marketing's Catalyst), and when the program is ready to be implemented, might look like this:

Promotion Manager	
communicates program	Communicator
↓	↓
Sales manager	Receiver
Sales Manager	Communicator
↓	↓
Regional sales management	Receiver
Each Regional Sales Manager	Communicator
↓	↓
Regional sales force	Receiver
Each Regional Sales Person	Communicator
↓	↓
Distributor principals	Receiver
Each Distributor Principal	Communicator
↓	↓
Distributor sales force	Receiver
Each Distributor Sales Person	Communicator
↓	↓
Retailer principals	Receiver
Each Retailer	Communicator
↓	↓
Consumers	Receiver and buyer

The sales promotion specialists and their organization, the marketing services agency, seek to solve problems in a number of marketing areas:

The Sales Force Even though each sales force is paid to sell, sales personnel must be made constantly more effective and motivated so that they will become more excited about selling the marketer's product. Therefore, each sales force must be given as much attention as any other marketing concern.

Sales Communication Sales personnel must be consistently convinced to do what the marketer wants them to do. How the marketer communicates with the salespeople relative to product promotion will affect their participation.

Trade Receptivity The marketer's various buying constituents must be interested. They will need extra benefits to help them sell the product.

Retail Support The marketer will need unique merchandising activities to help the retailer in terms of completing the sale.

Consumer Awareness The marketer will need additional attention mechanisms aside from controlled media to instill a greater product awareness in the minds of the buying public.

Product Differences The marketer must have value additions to the product to create a product different from those of competitors.

Positioning The marketer must provide advantage to the retailer in order to gain greater product visibility in the store.

Advertising Effectiveness To make controlled media more effective, the marketer must provide the retailer with ways to utilize a product's advertising to maximize in-store exposure.

Virtually all aspects of the marketplace, then, comprise the environment for sales promotion. From this we may say that

Sales promotion is an organized marketing activity.

Further:

Sales promotion is an organized marketing activity that motivates to a predictable action those people who influence the sale of a product or service.

In addition,

Sales promotion is the development and implementation of organized marketing activities that generate predetermined actions by specified audiences or publics within a designated period.

The three significant elements, it should be noted, are these:

An Organized Marketing Activity Promotion should be approached with the same energy and discipline that accompanies any critical marketing activity.

Specified People or Public The needs and expectations of every person involved in the distribution chain must be analyzed and addressed.

A Predetermined Action The desired result should be clearly identified in advance.

None of this says that promotion is coupons, or motivation, or point-of-sale displays, or product literature. It says, in effect, that *promotion is action; promotion is the business of moving people to an action that you want them to perform.* That action is clearly identifiable and clearly traceable; it is, in fact, both tangibly and intangibly measurable (see pages 36–39 for tangible and intangible elements in the marketing mix). The marketer can tell very soon whether a promotion has been successful.

In view of the tasks to be performed in the channels of distribution, it is easy to see why sales promotion is so extraordinarily complicated. *Everyone* influences the sale of a product or service—the sales force, the trade all along the distribution chain, and ultimately the consumer.

These definitions are not tactical ones. They do *not* refer to idea-effectiveness (because one good idea is not necessarily effective in every instance) but to action-effectiveness. The definitions suggest that business people should do something effective, not that they should do something different. Idea-effectiveness involves using the right tactics for the right situation.

A further complication of sales promotion is the industry's failure or reluctance to view a product as others see it, to look at it from the different perspectives of each person in the distribution chain.

To the marketer's product manager, Product X may be the only item for which he is responsible. His attention is focused on Product X; his efforts are devoted entirely to Product X.

For the company salesperson, broker salesperson, and distributor, however, Product X may be only one of many company products they are responsible for selling. Their attention is dispersed among the company's products, and their efforts are divided accordingly.

For the headquarters buyer, Product X is one item in a category of 15 to potentially hundreds of products. Since there may be as many as three dozen different categories, Product X may be one of 2,700 items. His perspective is inevitably very different from that of the company that manufactures Product X.

The store manager sees Product X as only one item out of perhaps 10,000 on his shelves, and merchandising 9,999 other items besides Product X is only one of his responsibilities.

In the eyes of the consumer, Product X is one of millions. Product X may get a fraction of a second of attention if any at all.

If Product X has made its way successfully through the various channels of distribution, it will finally be confronted by a wide range of products all vying for the consumer's attention. The way to cut through this clutter is to choose promotional tactics that best fit the strategy established for Product X and then to develop the creative concepts that best implement those tactics.

THE CONCEPT OF DELICATE BALANCE...
THE BUDGET

One of the most obviously difficult problems marketing directors face is finding a delicate balance, the best mix, between advertising and promotion expenditures. There is no convenient formula to determine which portion of the budget should go to advertising and which should go to promotion since each function is vastly different from the other.

These difficulties, traditionally, have been circumvented by a "historical" approach to budgeting. In this approach, a company merely creates a new budget that roughly conforms to previous years' budgets. This approach does not allow for changes in the marketplace. It assumes no changes in competitive activity or consumer perceptions will occur. It avoids the critical audit of the current marketing situation and predetermines the tactics that will be used regardless of the marketing climate. This "historical" approach can be likened to choosing clothing without regard to the temperature—obviously an ill-advised action at least a good part of the time.

A more suitable approach is neither simple nor historical, but requires a thorough understanding of selling as a two-dimensional concept that creates a synergistic relationship between advertising and promotion.

There are two dimensions to the sale of a product—(1) the *intangible* dimension, which involves advertising and what it creates (awareness, image, and attitude) and (2) the *tangible* dimension, which involves promotion and the specific actions associated with it (selling, displaying, and buying). Each can have a significant impact on the other.

To achieve an appropriate balance between advertising and promotion expenditures—the *intangible* and *tangible* marketing activities—it is necessary to follow general (although certainly not infallible) procedures. For purposes of illustration, assume that the products in question are at relative parity in price, package, and type with the rest of the marketplace.

We must first audit the *intangible* aspects of the brand. What do consumers think of the brand? How do they relate to it? Are they aware of it? If the brand is relatively unknown, then emphasis must be placed on intangibles. The budget must be weighted heavily toward advertising, with additional stress put on trade activities. Second, we must audit the *tangibles;* that is, identify the strengths and weaknesses of the selling organization. If the sales force is poorly informed, poorly trained, or poorly organized, or if it exhibits any other deficiencies, the budget should be weighted to correct these problems.

Contrary to normal expectations, tangible problems are more difficult to diagnose than intangible ones. Tangible problems are often quite complex and easily overlooked. A sales organization, for instance, often needs more than a good brand to sell. It might need better training and tools; it might require a better understanding of a brand's needs. Example: a marketer was faced with shrinking usage of the company's co-op advertising fund. Analysis revealed that the sales force did not know how to use the fund or create retail advertising. The marketer solved this tangible problem by creating new tools and training the sales force in the use of these tools. By providing the sales force with enough information to help the dealer put together local advertising programs the marketer achieved a significant increase in co-op fund usage and a 20 percent increase in sales.

Companies too frequently take their tangible marketing activities for granted and assume that, because the programs are in place, they are being used and understood and that they are benefiting sales and distribution. Unless such a marketing audit is conducted, and unless funds are properly budgeted, there is no guarantee that tangible marketing needs are being met.

Distribution, another tangible need, must be audited. If direct selling is involved, a company must determine if there is an appropriate number of retail outlets. Are they in the right classes of trade? Is the product generally available to the consumer?

If a company sells to a distributor organization, that firm's ability must be audited. Does it have an adequate sales force? Is the distributor's territory covered effectively? Does it have relationships with leading retailers? Is it financially stable, and does it provide the retailer with an appropriate financing plan? Does the distributor's sales force understand the product line?

Consider the importance of these questions in a practical example. A company with a two-step distribution system had difficulty with declining market shares. It eventually determined that the distributor organization had not kept pace with the retailers' changing financial needs and that it had not provided appropriate financing programs to accommodate those needs. As a solution, the company implemented a financial management package and offered various financial systems to both the distributor and the trade, together with the necessary training and selling tools. These new financial systems became critically important sales tools for the sales force and the distributor. The solution soon turned the number two product line into number one, and the company became a market leader and innovator.

The needs of the retailer must also be audited. A company was introducing a new line of products. An audit revealed that, although the product line was competitive with other products, the retailer had no way to display or demonstrate the product. To remedy this problem, a significant portion of the budget, more than 50 percent, was devoted to developing merchandising display tools. This unusual budgetary allocation allowed the company to dominate the market for three years. Even though competing products were of equal or greater quality, they could not be demonstrated on a retail level.

And then there are consumer needs. How does a company increase the odds of consumers buying the product? Intangible needs must be evaluated. If awareness, attitude, and image factors are lacking, then advertising should receive the greater share of the budget. If those factors are strong, however, then a substantial portion of the marketing dollar should be channeled into sales action-generating activities, the tangibles.

Among tangible marketing activities are certain, standard promotional tactics that involve premiums, couponing, games, and contests. Less direct incentives include point-of-sale displays, "worthy cause" activities, product sampling, demonstrations, and other consumer action-generating activities.

Need alone must determine how marketing dollars are spent; both tangible and intangible marketing needs must be audited. If only one is audited—if, for example, advertising recall and awareness scores are the only elements analyzed—an unbalanced budget will result. Auditing tangible needs is especially important because too frequently a sales organization, distributor, and retailer are overlooked in the process.

Dollars have to be funneled into programs for those three groups; if they aren't involved in the marketing process, don't have the tools, or don't understand how to make the process work, the program will be less successful than it should be.

Even if a huge budget is allocated for advertising, a product will not sell if the retailer is burying the product in a back aisle. A good advertising campaign can be a key to motivating the sales force. A superior promotion can turn advertising awareness into sales action.

Such a budgeting procedure is certainly far more complex than the historical approach. By investing the time and energy necessary to understand its own true marketing needs, a company can unravel these complex issues and create a marketing program that addresses them effectively.

CHAPTER 4

Promotion: Marketing's Arena for Future Research and Development

The most significant and often discouraging characteristic of marketing today is parity. It pervades the marketplace. Parity in product advertising and promotion is being created by parity people. They have created parity from a product point of view, from an advertising point of view, and certainly from a promotion point of view.

This phenomenon is the brainchild of today's marketing professional. Who is this professional? He is the man who has been trained to play it safe. She is the woman who has been trained to interpret the research in the same way everyone else interprets it. He has been trained about sales concepts as everyone else has been trained about sales concepts. She is trained about distribution, display, and pricing; and she is trained through her exposure and experience. Each is, as a consequence, exactly like all other contemporaries.

We are reminded of a story attributed to Procter & Gamble. A number of years ago, P&G instituted a policy of recruiting and hiring properly motivated people who came from the right kinds of backgrounds and the right kinds of schools and who sought the right kinds of success for themselves. After being interviewed extensively, these people became the executive trainees who were to achieve middle management positions in the Procter & Gamble organization.

One day, so the story goes, the company was faced with a major marketing problem concerning a category of product. Management decided to utilize this army of young MBAs, all of whom fit the mold. Management presented them with the problem and asked them to think about it and come back with a creative solution. When they all came back with the same solution, Procter & Gamble suddenly recognized that it had made a mistake.

That same army is out there today. They are working in key brand management spots. They are working for agencies that have limited tangible experience and that are endeavoring to manipulate an art and convert it to a science. Promotion, marketing, and selling, as well as advertising, are all art forms, not sciences. We cannot read the research and identify exactly how to respond to it. Not every consumer will react the same way to every coupon or every price promotion. We must disrupt this status quo, break out of this follow-the-leader mentality.

The problem seems to arise from a desperate fear of making a mistake. No one wants to be put in a position of innovating because "it has never been done before." In the minds of these young executives, the risks of attacking old problems with new ideas are greater than the potential rewards. As a result, decisions are made by people who have the same background. From a historical viewpoint, this is an extreme irony because the great consumer product corporations were not built by such marketing techniques.

Parity is caused in large part by *creative myopia*—a condition contracted by advertising creative people. These people become enamored of a style or an idea, and they race to see who can best execute that one idea. They stick to their pet style or idea regardless of the product, the audience, or the need. Instead of trying to broaden their skills by testing new ideas, by meeting new people, or by identifying new concepts, they seem compelled by their fear of failure and by their need for proof to do exactly what someone else has done in the past. Parity people, suffering from creative myopia, have created product parity.

Consider, for example, the issue of creativity. Many big advertising agencies rush to the big-name creative people on the justification that they have "used the best" to produce the very highest quality commercials they can for their clients. Instead of buying quality creativity, they are in fact buying reputation.

What is really needed are people with new and fresh experience—enlightened risk takers who have enough good sense to control the risk. So long as the quest for quality is dominated by the fear of failure, breakthroughs will inevitably come from the promotion side of the business, where risk is an inherent part of the day-to-day activity, where there is a realistic balance between the pursuits of art and science.

It is interesting to note some of the breakthrough ideas that have surfaced over the past few years and where they have come from:

Free Standing Insert Referred to as FSI, this is one of the most frequently used ideas in the last decade. The FSI was created as a *promotion* device to deliver coupons.

The Worthy Cause Originally created to separate a third-rate brand from the market leaders, this is a *promotion* that provides the reason for a retailer to promote.

Olympic Sponsorship This strategy was converted to a store traffic-building *promotion*. For the first time, a major media event was used to build retail traffic. Up to that point, the Olympics and that type of tie-in were simply a tag line in a piece of advertising.

Telemarketing This idea in general and the 800 number specifically were response techniques to a *promotion*.

These are typical of the new thinking, of the fresh ideas, of the risky kinds of concepts that have come essentially from the promotion side. In the future, in all likelihood, promotion will continue to dominate such ideas, however risky at first. These ideas, of course, will represent a kind of threat to advertising agency income and commission structures, which, as we know, are functions of media purchased.

Marketing people will probably remain reluctant to recommend risky tactics or ideas. Many young people in marketing management are so desperately concerned with their individual futures that they have neither the time nor the inclination to be inventive and creative. It is therefore incumbent on the promotion community to develop the new thinking, to create the new ideas, and to keep pace with the changing economic, social, and political environments that demand promotional innovation.

CHAPTER 5

Promotion: Marketing's Catalyst

As emphasized in Chapter 3, the success of a sales promotion program relies heavily not only on the shaping and funding of an idea, but also on the energy, involvement, and commitment of people *beyond* the idea. These relationships are all characteristics of the promotion process.

Promotion pulls together advertising, marketing, brand management, operations, and production—all the elements of human media in this broad internal process (see Figure 5–1). Promotion is the only discipline within the marketing department that is totally interdependent on all of the other disciplines. To handle the promotion function and organization successfully, you must know a great deal about what is going on in the company, especially in terms of the product and the marketing objectives behind the brand, how the product is sold, its distribution, and its availability. All those different marketing disciplines must fit into one cohesive, executable idea, and to that degree there is little question that

FIGURE 5–1

Promotion—Marketing's Catalyst

Manufacturing/Production/Purchasing
- schedule production
- supply need

Financing
- price
- allocate recources

Consumer
- buy
- guarantee
- usage manuals

Packaging
- develop package
- consumer, trade, wholesale

Aisle clerk/Retail sales
- sales tools
- training
- information

Advertising
- communicate benefits
- create awareness
- reinforce image

Promotion Department

Sales force
- sales tools
- training
- meetings
- trade shows

Marketing
- identify needs
- position and market product
- create the deal
- segment market

Retailer
- display
- sell
- service

Product development
- create the product that fills the needs

Distributor/Wholesaler
- warehouse
- sell
- finance
- distribute
- promote

promotion's role in the marketing department is that of a catalyst.

People who do not come to grips with this fact frequently find themselves creating promotions that are well-conceived, that are absolutely right for the category at the right time, but that are 100 percent wrong in terms of distribution or the company's production capabilities.

In order to perform effectively, either as a sales promotion manager or as a promotion department manager, you must be involved in all the marketing components of your company. The promotion professional, similarly, so deeply involved in the client's business that he understands every aspect of the communication-reception link, recognizes this fact; and it is his company, the marketing services agency, not just a promotion agency, that understands the role of promotion relative to the development and creation of the promotion idea. It is able, if necessary, to work effectively in at least five broad disciplines within the client's company: (1) product development, (2) marketing management, (3) advertising, (4) sales, and (5) manufacturing and distribution.

What, more specifically, is the involvement of the promotion manager himself in these disciplines? He must be involved with product development people to understand the rationale behind the development of the new product and its components. He must be involved with and understand the marketing people responsible for the packaging, the positioning, identifying the level of investment, and providing the focus to the market and its segments where this new product would fit. He must understand that, with this information in hand, the advertising agency and people create the consumer message and identify the media that will best reach that market or market segment as defined by the marketing department.

He must then know that sales has to ensure that it has the staff or the structure in place and trained, ready to begin the process of selling this product. Manufacturing and distribution must then produce enough product in a timely fashion and put together the distribution system to deliver the product to the ultimate consumer or distributor in an effective, cost-efficient manner.

The promotion manager *must* interact with all these people. If he does not know how and why the product is positioned the way it is or the extent of the investment behind the product, he will have to make these decisions himself—a superfluous, if not plain silly, exercise, particularly if the work has already been done.

Funding, or the way in which the manager can support the product at retail, is an important component of budgeting. It is important that the manager knows what that category has done in the past, what the marketing department anticipates as success targets for the product, and what the greatest potential segments of the market are. All this information helps the manager identify the kinds of programs needed. For example, if the target market were teenagers, a manager might look at types of promotion that focused on music or school involvement where the core of the promotion idea involved the teenage lifestyle. If, on the other hand, the target market included senior citizens, he might view the promotion in terms of recreational or crafts activities or better ways for seniors to utilize their time or funds.

If there is an advertising message or advertising positioning to coordinate with, he must know what the advertising is saying and what brand image the advertising is trying to create. He will then build the sales tools and the support materials that are compatible with, though not necessarily identical to, that creative positioning.

The manager must be familiar with the sales organization's structure, capabilities, and available time so that he can provide sales with the tools necessary to bring the promotion into focus for the distributor and the trade.

He must deal with manufacturing in order to know what the production schedules are, what kind of packing will be done, and what kind of distribution systems will exist. Will the product be shipped to farthest markets first? Or will it be shipped to in-markets first?

Besides familiarity with these areas of knowledge, he must have some production skills in both graphic arts and physical production. Promotion people in many companies lack these qualities. In fact, the promotion manager is often promoted from sales. Lack of these communication skills in the early stages of a manager's development is a serious problem. However, it is even more serious if management does not understand the importance of the job and is not sympathetic to the scope of the promotion manager's responsibilities.

The promotion manager's qualifications and credentials are as important as his acute awareness of the problems of promotion management. Although education is desirable, *undoubtedly the most important qualifications are experience and the innate ability to learn from experience.*

The key to being a good promotion manager, and a good catalytic agent, as well as the key to being a good executive, lies in the capacity to empathize with each discipline and to ask the right questions at the right times. Not only with details peculiar to one specific business, but to any details involving graphics. The manager should be surrounded by a team of specialists ready for any contingency.

The lack of collective expertise in companies' promotion departments is a major problem: the lack of specialized talents and/or knowledge inhibits learning from experience. Personnel often fail to recognize what might be needed for each subsequent promotion and thereby do not anticipate special situations when they arise.

Suppose that a national fast food chain wants to plan a promotion involving french fries. No matter how good the promotion could be—projecting its potential against past records of similar promotions—if the promotion manager positions it when the potato crop is at its lowest and fails to plan with the purchasing department to have enough potatoes on hand, there is no way the promotion will succeed. Fast food chains consume enormous amounts of potatoes throughout the year. The additional amount needed for a special promotion would only increase that already-high demand.

As a broader illustration, suppose a manufacturer offered a cents-off label promotion. The implications of this promotion touch almost everyone in the organization.

Ample product production lead time is essential.

Sufficient availability of product must be assured.

Labeling and/or special packaging must be completed.

New cartons must be on hand; they have to be ordered, manufactured, and printed.

Sales sheets and other information-conveying tools have to be created, printed, and distributed.

People who do the packing and shipping must work ahead.

Warehousing of the product (in the distribution chain) must precede the promotion because special packaging may be supported with media; media exposure and product availability must break at the same time.

Code numbers must be established for the retailers so that they can take delivery before the media announce the promotion.

Assume this promotion *is* to be media-supported. The critical questions for the promotion manager are (*a*) How much time will the sales force need to cover its territories? (*b*) How much product is already in the pipeline and how much time will be needed to clear it out? and (*c*) What is a legitimate time period to allow all of the cents-off product to be in place before the advertising in support of that program can appear on the networks or in the local markets? When will the special product be on the retailer's shelf? Unless the promotion manager acts with the knowledge and the good faith of the sales, manufacturing, and distribution people, product may be delivered too late or too early, making the media totally ineffectual.

Any interruption in timing anywhere could ruin the promotion. The promotion manager and his team must work smoothly with all departments of the company and encourage each department's cooperation in meeting deadlines. The manager must also work with all the human media in the marketing chain.

PROMOTION MAY *NOT* BE
MARKETING'S PANACEA

Despite promotion's critically important role as a marketing catalyst and its indispensable role in marketing success, promotion, by itself, can be a victim of its own effectiveness. The frequently startling sales results of a promotion tactic can too easily seduce marketers into believing that the idea itself is great. Marketers often view the successful result without considering the ingredients that made it successful. They fail to recognize promotion's need for involvement and support of all the people in the marketing/sales spectrum, from the top marketing executive to the local aisle clerk.

While it is true that "The Great Promotion Idea" can periodically produce very attractive sales results, almost invariably the dramatic success is short-lived. As marketing consultant Robert M. Prentice has concluded in his case studies:

> They [too many marketers] are not using the proper advertising/promotion mix. They are putting too much emphasis on certain types of promotion that have only a short-term effect on sales (and are *high* in ultimate cost) and not enough on advertising and certain other types of promotion that

have a cumulative impact on sales for about four years (at a far lower relative cost).[1]

Working with the Marketing Science Institute (see page 23), Prentice developed an analytical marketing technique in which he designated certain activities as *Consumer Franchise Building* (CFB) and other activities as *Non-Consumer Franchise Building* (Non-CFB).[2]

He based the CFB concept in part on "(1) convincing the consumer that a particular brand provides unique and important advantages (value) over competitive products; (2) making the brand readily available for purchase; and (3) offering occasional short-term incentives to accelerate the buying decision. . . . Advertising is the most common CFB activity."[3] He made a further distinction by referring to all consumer promotions and all trade deals as Non-CFB activities. These particular activities accelerate the buying decision by:

> (1) reducing the price temporarily, or (2) offering an extraneous incentive, such as a premium or contest, or (3) helping to obtain trade distribution and featuring. Non-CFB promotions do *not* implant ideas [in the mind] about a brand's unique qualities. (A cut price is seldom unique. A trade deal—essential as it is—does not deliver any message to the consumer about a brand's unique attributes.)[4]

Prentice's results were based on case histories of brands from over 40 companies collected over a period of 10 to 15 years each. They illustrate some practical guidelines for marketers searching for a proper advertising/promotion mix and put in sharp perspective the inadvisability of concentrating on promotion tactics themselves. In part, he concluded:

1. CFB activities (advertising and a few promotions that work like advertising) have a *cumulative impact on sales for about four years.*
2. Non-CFB activities (primarily price promotions, trade deals, and most FSI couponing) affect sales for *only a year or less.*
3. CFB activities are thus relatively low in ultimate cost, while Non-CFB activities are relatively *high* in cost over the long term.

4. When a brand spends too much on short-term, high-cost, Non-CFB activities at the expense of long-term, low-cost CFB activities, *profits almost always decline within two years....*

5. Continued imbalance between CFB and Non-CFB expenditures erodes marketing productivity and profit....continued overemphasis on Non-CFB price promotions and trade deals practically eliminates the four-year cumulative impact of CFB activities and is actually counterproductive.

6. Successful brands split their money between CFB and Non-CFB activities (especially trade promotion) in a long-term pattern that is exactly the opposite of the pattern followed by unsuccessful brands. The key to success is keeping a brand's share of category spending for each type of activity in the proper relationship to its market share....

7. A simple CFB "Rule of Thumb" formula closely approximates a brand's share of market by adding five numbers together and dividing by four. Using a brand's shares of CFB and Non-CFB expenditures over a four-year period, this simple formula provides an 80+ percent correlation with actual market share.[5]

Part II

The Promotion Process

CHAPTER 6

Information Gathering and Planning...
Where It All Begins

PROMOTION PHILOSOPHY

Companies that are successful in their use of promotion have recognized the need to develop their own philosophies for the role promotion is to play in their marketing programs. They know that only concerted action turns a marketing plan into a marketing accomplishment. They know that, in marketing, the forces of personal selling, advertising, promotion, and merchandising combine to move a product through the channels of distribution and into the hands of consumers.

Just as these companies establish marketing objectives and advertising philosophies to create brand image, attitude, and awareness, so do they, in the same spirit, establish an overriding promotion goal. This does not refer simply to generating sales but rather to a broad, clear definition of the role of promotion in the total marketing plan—a role especially compatible in personality with advertising, product positioning, and packaging. This is the *promotion philosophy* for the brand in the total marketing mix; it states that promotion's role should be more than simply trade or sales support.

Some go so far as to develop a written statement of philosophy, subject to yearly review when deemed necessary by changing market conditions. The promotion philosophy is then used specifically as a guideline for establishing the role of the individual promotional ideas and executions developed throughout the year.

Media and nonmedia programs may then work harmoniously to reach the overall marketing objectives; and promotion can have a definite impact on brand image, or it can help improve the brand's consumer franchise and position.

KNOW THE MARKETING PLANS

The indispensable ingredient in the beginning is *complete* knowledge of the company's marketing plans. What are the company's future plans for the brand? What is it attempting to do with advertising? What is it attempting to do with distribution? What are its various marketing activities, both long- and short-term? Creating a promotion that is poorly timed and inconsistent with all other marketing activity is difficult but possible, as we explored briefly in Part I.

A 12-month advertising campaign, for example, which is designed to build a brand image of quality and value, can be rendered virtually useless if it is followed by a heedless and sloppy price promotion that contradicts what the company says in its advertising.

The issue is one of *consistency of the whole*. The longer a brand is established, the more validity its image possesses, *and* the more predictable the consumer's attitude will be toward it. The strength of the *brand image* depends on the consumer's attitude toward the brand: "I, as a consumer, expect such-and-such from this brand."

National brands are constantly image-building, and they spend a great deal of money to do so through their advertising. It is often a marketing irony, however, that some companies that devote heavy advertising efforts to building brand image are "hard-nosed" merchandisers. "Hard-nosed" merchandising consists of sales promotion tactics at the retail level that are inconsistent with advertising but are absolutely correct for building sales at retail. Let's say, for example, that when one buys laundry equipment made by Maytag, he expects that it will be dependable and he will have no serious service problems. It will wash and dry his clothes. How does he know this? Because the company's advertising has for years told him so; and it is true. The quality is very high, and he has to pay more for it.

The Maytag Company understands two things that are quite different: the function of promotion and (not confusing it with) the function of advertising. Maytag does the "20-kids-in-one-family-and-my-Maytag-is-still-running" ad. In this particular campaign the head of the house exclaims: "I mean, it's just dependability... it just goes on forever. It's still working. I bought it when my first child was born. I now have six kids and that beauty is still running, and I do seven loads of wash a day." And then Maytag does the lonely repairman: "I have nothing to do. I'm a Maytag repairman. I live here all by myself, and nobody comes to visit me. My only joy in life is talking to my mother on the telephone." Maytag's advertising stresses strongly the durability and dependability of its products.

The Maytag Company recognizes, however, that the retail business is different from the brand business. The retail objective is to get buyers in the store and to sell them something. To do this, Maytag dealers use every tactic available—price leaders, rebates, coupons; you name it, they will use it. And the corporation that has practiced all this media theory—strong, image-building advertising—also has used extremely short-term, competition-challenging, newspaper price-off, and price-cutting promotions.

Does all this *hurt* the brand image? According to Maytag, it apparently does not because retailers say they want and need these promotions. Maytag gives retailers what they want, but it does not confuse the needs of the retailers with the needs of the brand. Retailers rely on the advertiser (Maytag Company) to build an image, and Maytag has consistently done a fine job. Maytag's success as advertiser is crucial to the retailer since the consumer associates the promotion with the retailer, not with the Maytag Company.

At the same time, the company does not go to the retailer and say, "We'd like you to advertise our brand at retail the same way we advertise it nationally." Were the company to

do that, the retailer, in all likelihood, would tell the marketing management to go fly a kite. *All concerned must understand the objectives.*

Ironically, then, this tactic is not destructive. Quite the opposite. Everyone recognizes that there are different tactics
for different needs. Everyone understands that those big,
schlocky banners hanging in the store that read, "Save on
Maytag!" "Limited Offer!" or whatever the retailer wants,
are what will be used.

Even with these tactics, Maytag can sell for a *higher* price
than its competitors—even without a rebate—because of the
brand image. A retailer's banner reading, "$50 Off On A
Maytag," is much more meaningful than "$50 Off On An
XYZ Brand" because Maytag has the quality image. If the
consumer can save $50 on an XYZ Brand washer/dryer, he
certainly should be pleased, but if he can save $50 on a super-
quality Maytag product, he should be more pleased. This is
true even though the consumer will pay substantially more
for the Maytag.

The preeminent position of the Maytag brand consequently
allows the manufacturer to do what many companies cannot
do. Maytag's performance, moreover, is a rarity in what
otherwise might be considered an inconsistent marketing
practice. With good advertising, some authorities maintain,
tactics such as price-off and price-cutting promotions should
not be necessary, and their market research supports this position, according to William T. Moran, president of Moran,
Inc., a market research company.

Moran states that

> ...advertising supports and supplements the consumer's
> perceptions and experiences with the brand and places a
> value on it. With advertised brands...consumers frame
> opinions "as to how and when the product fits into their
> lives." As price promotions affect sales, "a fully successful
> advertising campaign will make more people willing to pay
> full price for the brand and less likely to accept a competitive
> price incentive." ...[t]he ad campaign "also will make addi-
> tional people more willing to buy the brand at a small in-
> creased price incentive over competition," since advertising
> had enabled consumers to place a value on the product and
> judge a bargain offer.[1]

For some, sales promotion then suffers another setback in its reputation because its efforts seem counterproductive to the advertising agency's ongoing task of promoting a strong brand image. Fortunately, however, management still recognizes the need for effective sales promotion.

How can this happen? It can happen because management is frequently guilty of not giving sales promotion professionals all the information necessary to create a promotion compatible with the brand image. "We are sharing all this information with our advertising agency and *they* are counseling us," is the attitude. "We don't need to share it with others. The agency is the keeper of our image, and we'll just tell the others what we want."

One of the major benefits of promotion is that it has short-term impact and can generate results in a relatively short period. To that degree, *short-term* is an appropriate description of some promotions. On the other hand, promotion has or can have very serious long-term implications. If the wrong strategy or tactics are used, all other work relative to the brand and its credibility to the trade and to the sales force can suffer; the wrong promotion can do irreparable damage to the distribution system. Sensitivity to long-term implications and knowledge of the corporate plan are crucial elements in planning any promotion.

An integral part of that planning is knowledge of all the people who will be involved in the promotion; you must know their capabilities and their limitations. Any incorrect assumptions about the sales organization, the trade, or the consumer can lead to a promotion's failure. Everyone's money and energy will have been wasted.

Developing a feeling for the company involved will contribute to a good promotion. One must know what the company wishes to accomplish with a promotional activity and what the promotion's impact will be on the overall marketing plan.

People make up companies. Companies are not bloodless entities. Consider, for example, the four giants, Procter & Gamble, General Foods, Colgate-Palmolive, and Lever Brothers. Each has a large sales organization and many brand managers. One might think that they all work the same way since so many of the personnel come from similar backgrounds, right? Wrong.

These four companies are very different. They have different corporate personalities. They approach their markets differently. Their advertising is different. Their sales organizations are different. Their sales tools are different. Dealers react to them in different ways. Their products look different at retail.

A promotion put together for Procter & Gamble might work brilliantly for them, yet the same promotion might be a disaster for Lever Brothers because of that big difference in corporate personality. It makes no sense, therefore, to think that a brand can be fitted to a promotion ("We have four promotions...pick one."); the promotion must be tailored to the brand. And the promotional goals must be very clear.

Let's say that, in its marketing plan, a company has a clearly identified future for its brand in terms of line extension (new sizes, new product applications, and new features). Now, if what the marketing management sees is an *ever-expanding* brand in terms of what that product will do, or how the company will promote or merchandise the product, or how it will suggest the consumer use the product, then promotion for a short-term sales gain might be the worst thing marketing management could do. Perhaps management should try to gain visibility for that brand on the shelf and temporarily disregard sales volume (having enough product movement, of course, to ensure shelf space).

From that point, the company should attempt to measure that visibility and to measure how the consumer or the trade is going to get involved in that brand. It thereby lays the groundwork for future activity in the months or years ahead. Research findings might suggest that the company expand sizes, expand features, or expand usage recommendations. Without careful overall planning, marketing management's big cents-off effort, for example, might merely make its brand another parity product along with all other competitive products. The brand might simply become another price brand, and the integrity of marketing management's long-term brand plan would evaporate.

A key example of this principle lies in the Jergen's Lotion story. This brand was supposed to perform at retail like a product from P&G, Lever Brothers, Colgate, or General Foods; but it was not like one of those products and it could not perform as they do. The problem for Jergen's Lotion management was how to demonstrate to its sales force and to the trade, through various marketing mechanisms management was to have set up, that the company meant what it said when referring to its product's high quality. Furthermore, it had to relay the message in a convincing way. Jergens failed because it did not take those first appropriate steps in planning a good promotion: (1) conveying to its promotion people what the marketing plan was and (2) furnishing them with sufficient background information and clearly identifying what it wanted to accomplish at both the trade and consumer levels. The result was a poorly prepared sales force and no trade confidence in the brand.

The background information and the marketing information come from the client. Clients must say to those whose help they have enlisted, "Here is what we want to get done, here are the caveats, here are the criteria against which we can measure our efforts."

As was discussed earlier, the marketing services agency has only recently become involved in developing the marketing plan. After a long-term relationship with the client, the agency becomes an integral part of the marketing-planning function. That marketing service agents are becoming integral to the corporate marketing plan is evidence that certain clients feel that the concept is viable. They see that nonmedia people are as important to them as media people, and they can see this only after a long and productive relationship.

Many client advertisers have finally realized that the marketing services agency must know a great deal about their businesses in order to develop sound strategies and creative ideas. This is not to say that the marketing services agency does not include the media in the marketing plan; to the contrary, after the strategies have been determined, after the creative ideas have been generated, those involved in the marketing plan go to the media (through the advertising agency, of course) and say, "Media, execute your parts of the plan."

The distinct advantage here is that the media do execute their plan, and they *guarantee* it.

Promotion, quite differently, relies heavily on human media (see Chapter 3 on Definitions and Concepts). That is why the marketing services agency must know so much about the media.

It must know what the salespeople do and what they are capable of doing.

It must know sales management's perspective on the business.

It must know what the distributor's needs are and how it can fulfill them with what is to be accomplished.

It must know the distributor's sales representatives and what motivates them.

It must know what problems are faced by the trade level people, especially the trade level salespeople; and it must know what they are looking for and what motivates them.

These are the human media, those individuals who will be involved with getting that message, that idea, that concept from the marketer through all the channels of distribution to the consumer in a way that is understandable and workable to the consumer. Unless these human needs of human media are satisfied—satisfied by adequate background information and enough understanding of the various distribution elements—an inadequately prepared promotion may go awry. No product, no point in the distribution chain is free from this risk.

Reliance on human needs is what makes promotional planning so labor-intensive (and it is this characteristic that makes so many people reluctant to become involved in promotional planning... "I don't want to work that hard"). In advertising, an individual gets an idea, and the agency executes it and buys the media. In promotion, the individual gets the idea, executes it, and then makes certain that it is properly implemented every point along the way. Promotion is obviously more labor-intensive because of the energy required of the sales force, of the trade, and of the distributors.

Miller Brewing Company's experience, like that of all beer companies, illustrates this perfectly. A proper promotion for this company is directed as much at the driver-salesperson as at the consumer. In fact, it is directed more at him because if he does not like what has been prepared, he will never take it off his truck. The promotion can include the world's greatest idea; but if the driver-salesperson does not like pink, let us say, what can anyone do about it? Nothing. So it behooves the promotional team to know how the driver-salesperson feels about his job, his role in relation to the company, and his customers.

A certain incentive saver stamp company is an excellent illustration of a company whose promotion can lose its effectiveness altogether. Its marketing services agency accepted the word of some management personnel about the purported sophistication of its sales force. The agency delivered the promotional program to the company's management, which then turned it over to the sales force. Result? The program failed because the agency, accepting management's assessment of its sales force's capabilities, failed to go through the appropriate investigative stage on its own to determine what the sales personnel really knew and what they could and would do in their interactions with their customers. The agency discovered, contrary to what management said, that the salespeople were simply order takers.

The salespeople typically walked into the stamp subscriber (a retail store) and said, "How many stamps do you want today? Here...let me fill up your machine. You should have 10 rolls of stamps in reserve, and you only have four. Therefore, you need six. Thank you very much." And it's off to the next call.

Salespeople had never been involved with the retailer's promotional needs or with building a solid business relationship between stamp company and retailer, nor were they prepared, apparently, to do so.

CHAPTER 7

Concept Development: Strategy—What to Do

The marketing services agency now knows what the marketer company wants to accomplish. It has acquired a sense of what the company is and what its relationships are in the marketplace. The agency consequently learns what its own staff has to accomplish, and it moves to the business of identifying what the concept must be to get everyone to perform the desired action.

What, then, is to be the strategy? What is it we are going to do? Whatever the idea and strategy, the agency, armed with information and understanding, now has "screens" to put those new ideas through to affect a projected effectiveness, like a kind of checkpoint list procedure to inform everyone that they may proceed with assurance.

In the instance of the stamp company, the plan was to merchandise their catalog, and the best strategy to accomplish that task was determined to have been a game promotion. The strategy was sound, and the idea of the game was extremely good, but the agency did not run the strategy through its "screens" and conclude that it would not work. Since management's word was accepted, there were, in effect, no "screens". Management should have known that it would not work, but it did not know. The agency could have easily considered a number of other strategies, but the one it selected was wrong for the client. What is worse is that the client was so out of touch with its sales force that it did not know that the strategy was wrong. With another, more sophisticated company the experience might have differed in two ways. The company might have known more about its own sales force, and the marketing services agency might have done a better investigative job regarding the people and their abilities to execute a promotion.

So, there they were, with a strategy the agency thought was marvelous, which under the right circumstances could have been brilliantly executed, but which was instead a gigantic flop.

An idea is frequently right if it can be understood by the sales force. If it cannot be executed who will care? The idea can be quite simple, it can be a "no-brainer," but if it works, it's the right idea.

Whatever the idea or the concept, in its development it must be measured against the background information. It must go through all the "screens"—the human screen, the strategic screen, the marketing screen, and the financial screen.

The idea need not necessarily be either good or bad because good and bad are not the issue. *Usefulness is the real issue.*

Can it be used?

Can it be executed?

Can the people in the field—all the human media involved in the idea—make it come alive?

Do they have enough information?

Do they have the background and experience?

Are they motivated?

Is the idea consistent with the way their performance is measured?

Is it too complicated?

Does it have built-in complications that make it impossible for the consumer to respond to?

The strategy must be dissected because it can be the weakest link in the product's distribution chain. When the idea ultimately gets to the consumer, it must be understandable, executable, and affordable.

New strategy development or concept development can only be initiated with all the appropriate background information. Had the stamp company's marketing services agency known that the sales force was unsuited for the promotion, it would either have submitted a different idea with a different strategy or it would have tried to convince the client to prepare the sales force properly to use the original strategy.

It seems obvious that a company would know the sales activities along the distribution chain, but even with the best of companies this is not always the case. A major TV manufacturer, after executing similar promotions for years, decided on a change of pace. Its promotion management knew that an appropriate strategy was not necessarily the most innovative or the freshest; rather, it was the one that could be executed. One year it decided to put its major effort and most of its promotion money into an incentive and motivation program for both retail levels (store buyers and salespeople) and wholesale levels (distributor sales representatives selling to retailers). It offered foreign travel for incremental sales and purchases over projection.

Both levels went wild, and in the last month before the six-month sales drive period was over, the race to place orders was without precedent; dealers tried to purchase enough to include additional salespeople, and wholesaler principals and salespeople tried to fill orders.

With this first-half momentum, the company put together its second-half production plans. Using the new sales trends, manufacturing began an accelerated production schedule, and the television sets poured off the assembly line. The result was a temporary disaster: the company failed to learn what the distributors and retailers were doing with the product. It did not realize that the product was not moving off the shelves at the same rate as it was moving onto the shelves. It did not discover, until too late, that the incentive was too lucrative. Everyone wanted a trip, so all participants purchased to the extent of necessary commitments and carried a larger than usual inventory.

During the first three months of the second half the manufacturer's sales plummeted. Product coming off the assembly line ended up in the warehouse. Management was dumbfounded. What was going on? What happened to their momentum? The economy was not that bad.

The strategy was to build and execute an incentive program, a strategy and concept developed in the short-term; and it worked wonderfully in terms of the criteria set down. At year-end, though, the company did not have one penny more in incremental sales than it did from the previous year. What is worse, it did not have one penny more than it would have if it had done nothing at all! Still worse, it had conducted a very expensive merchandising program whose costs reduced year-end profits.

The strategy was right for the short-term but produced negative results in the long-term. What served as short-term acceptance and success eventually proved to be long-term disaster. A company must ask itself what the long-term significance will be of any wonderful idea. If it decides to develop a creative concept and strategy, it must include a way to move merchandise to the consumer as well; otherwise, the concept is no more than a purchasing incentive for the trade. The trade will simply buy at its normal levels but alter the purchase pattern, buying more of its requirements earlier than usual. Misinterpretation of a market activity such as this can be costly, as was discovered.

Loading up the trade can be a legitimate part of a promotion strategy. The larger purpose, however, would be to lock out competition. This is a legitimate concept and strategy that is done on a regular basis. Part of the strategy in such a promotion might be to lower the price or add a purchase incentive of such magnitude during the promotional period that the trade has very little reason to buy the competition's product. It is a safe strategy as long as the promotion does not contain any false or misleading implications about sales momentum and as long as there is an executable sales plan to help the retailer move the product. It is simply a way to lock out competition while the promotion is being conducted.

The right strategy for a product that has a small market share is crucial if its promotion is to succeed against fierce, pervasive competition. Such was the experience of Dad's Root Beer in the big soft drink industry.

Dad's Root Beer is a small brand. It is considered a secondary brand in the bottling business—it is not a Coke, a Pepsi, or a 7UP. It generally rides in the wake of the bigger brands. Tied in with another product for a summer promotion, though, Dad's Root Beer did very well. The tie-in product was Orville Redenbacher's Popcorn. This small but successful Indiana popcorn company was just introducing a new buttery flavored popping oil. Dad's Root Beer offered a free sample of popcorn *and* the buttery popping oil (a 50-cent value) with every eight-pack of root beer (see Figure 7–1). "You buy the Dad's, we buy the popcorn and oil." This was an on-pack, value-added free premium at the point of sale.

FIGURE 7–1

Dad's Root Beer and Orville Redenbacher Popcorn Tie-in Promotion Kit

Courtesy of Hunt Wesson Foods, Inc.

In addition, Dad's arranged a Free Standing Insert coupon drop in key markets—a cents-off coupon for Dad's Root Beer, a coupon good for the popcorn, and a coupon good for the oil. This was a cooperative arrangement between Orville Redenbacher and Dad's, each promoting the other and each gaining considerable strength from the combined effort.

The promotion moved 2 million samples and, of course, a great volume of root beer. This would never have worked with Coke, for example, because Redenbacher could not have made enough popcorn. For a small brand like Dad's, however, the promotion was ideal, the marriage of the brands perfect, and the strategy absolutely correct. This is an example of how one strategy can be good for one product but not for another, even one in the same category.

The development of the concept is critical. Knowing what can be used and what cannot be used is a function of knowledge about the company, the sales force, the category, the brand, and the brand's distribution.

Suppose that, with the same concept, the strategy *was* to be used with Coke. First of all, it could help Coke sales. But because Coke, like Pepsi, gets price feature and display feature all the time, the strategy would be far too labor-intensive for Coke and too product-intensive for Orville Redenbacher. Coke might be willing to support the program in selected competitive regions, but Orville Redenbacher wants national distribution. The decision from the Redenbacher perspective centered on lower-level national support versus high-intensity regional support.

CHAPTER 8

Concept Development: Making the Creative Process Work

Once objectives and strategy are clear and once all concerned know what to do, the promotion, if it is to come to life, must now go to the creative people. How do you design the idea? How do you create the idea that will capture the imagination of everyone involved?

To be creative means to take a new approach to something, to render something differently, to put things together in a new way, to give a new meaning to something.

When clients buy creativity, they are buying unique ways to help merchandise and sell their products and services. To the sales promotion specialist, the terms *creative* and *creativity* usually refer to three basic elements of a promotion: (1) the *idea*, (2) the *copy*, and (3) the *graphics*. The idea is the core of the promotion; the words and the graphics communicate this idea to the intended audience.

Having a creative idea is often a matter of recognizing similarities or relationships, of drawing an analogy between one thing and another. There's the legend, for example, about Archimedes jumping out of a public bath in ancient Greece and running naked down the streets exclaiming about his most recent discovery: the principle of specific gravity. He had noticed that when he submerged himself in the bath water, a certain amount of water, equal in volume to that of his own body, was displaced and overflowed. He made a mental connection between taking a bath and the scientific measurement of solids.

In a contemporary context, we might make a similar kind of analysis: supermarkets attract large amounts of traffic with coupons for packaged goods, and an airline needs to rebuild its passenger traffic quickly after a long strike. Here was the unprecedented traffic-building idea for United Airlines' half-fare coupons, a technique no airline had ever used before. You cannot always hit the promotional jackpot as United Airlines did, but creativity can have a substantial influence on the effectiveness of incentive programs and traffic-building promotions.

In the creative process, the first two steps are closely related: (1) define the problem or objective as clearly as possible and (2) gather all the relevant information on the subject. Sometimes the definition of the problem will indicate what additional information is needed, and sometimes the information will indicate what the problem or objective is. Managers should not set too many objectives for the promotion. The more they try to accomplish, the more they will dilute the impact of the promotion, and the less it will actually achieve. An excessive number of objectives is an occupational hazard for the creative process. In sales promotion, less is more.

In the information-gathering process it is important to learn what solutions have already been used or suggested. Thinking up something that has already been thought of is a waste of valuable time. Nevertheless, you can take an old idea and use it as a starting point for a new idea. Perhaps that old idea can be twisted or added onto or somehow made new and better.

The keystone of creativity in sales promotion is *empathy*. An essential part of the input is an understanding of the target audience. Who is the client talking to with this promotion? What is going on in the heads of the audience? If a company wants to persuade its employees or its customers to do something, it must know them well enough to see things from their viewpoints. It must put itself into their shoes in order to anticipate the impact of its promotion.

When a marketing services agency takes on a creative problem, the people in the creative group assigned to that project will absorb all the information fed to them. They will analyze it, talk about it, juggle it in their heads until they are thoroughly familiar with it. Then they will forget about it for awhile. They may work on another project, do something else, go home, or sleep on it. In one way or another, they will get their conscious minds off the problem and allow their subconscious minds to take over. The problem is going through an incubation period.

After two days or so, the creative group is ready to begin thinking about the problem consciously. Now, as the creative people generate ideas, they must also *suspend any judgment* of them. Whatever they come up with comes out, and they do not allow themselves to be critical. They do not say among themselves, "No, that's no good; that won't work." They allow the ideas, or words, or graphic designs to flow freely. Never nipping an idea in the bud, they put *everything* down on paper no matter how wild or wrong it may seem at first glance. Nothing is suppressed. They indulge themselves in the process of free association, one thought leading to another. Sooner or later, they have a great number of ideas.

Then they begin to evaluate every idea. Some ideas may be insane, some may be considerably off target, some may be impractical. Some, though, will be good, workable ideas that are effective solutions to the original objectives. Some, however wrong in themselves, may point the way to a right approach. Some that start as jokes or ostensibly insane ideas may, after serious reconsideration, be very right for the objectives. Sometimes, on the other hand, none of the ideas will be good enough. Back they go to their typewriters and drawing boards until the right answers become evident.

If all goes well, they will eventually create a blockbuster of a promotional concept.

What this idea (or ideas) may be depends, of course, on the particular project. There are no generalizations. The idea may be for a promotional strategy, a tactic, a theme, or a graphic design. Whatever form the idea takes, the creative people must now develop the concept by creating the actual elements of the program. They must write the copy and design the graphics for each piece in the package.

Once again, the creative group must search for ideas. This time, the ideas must be for the best way to make the promotion relate its point to the target audience. This process involves writing, sharpening, and polishing the copy to express the idea with maximum clarity and persuasiveness. It involves designing eye-catching graphics that help communicate the message and enhance the image of the client company. Sometimes this phase goes well the first time, sometimes it still is not right the fifth time. The creative group pounds away at the problem until it is solved.

They always keep in mind that connection between creativity and effectiveness, the means to the end. There is continual emphasis on being as creative as possible to make the promotion as effective as possible.

The obligation for creativeness should not be limited to the creative department. Account service people can be a major source of creative marketing ideas. Research people can think of new ways of improving the data input that feeds the creative process. Direct response people can try new ways to improve the response rate for the client company.

The client company can contribute substantially to the creative process. It can help set a realistic, clearly defined objective. It can collect all the necessary background information that becomes the raw material for the creative mind. It can start work on a project with enough lead time for the creative process to generate the best answer. The client company can allow time for ideas to germinate, and to incubate, and to develop. It can allow time for all elements to be written, designed, and produced to the high standards it should expect from the marketing services agency. It can guarantee that there is enough time to judge the creative output according to the factor that counts the most—performance of the promotion in the marketplace and along the channels of distribution.

The better the client company makes the input, the better the creative output will be, and the more effective the marketing services agency will be within the constraints of time and money available to create the promotion.

For example, consider the International Harvester S-Series heavy-duty truck—the 9670. This is the best of the IH over-the-road trucks. It has two design configurations which are only cosmetically different. One is designed primarily for fleet buyers who own 10 or more trucks; the other is designed for owner-operators of one or two trucks. Owner-operators have a direct concern for creature comforts because they do the driving. Those cosmetic differences amount to optional equipment and features (whistles, bells, extra lights, stereo, etc.), and in a way they can be compared to the differences between driving a Chevrolet and a Cadillac. The mechanical workings of the trucks are the same: the guts are the same, the engine is the same, the wheels are the same, the drive trains are the same, the transmissions are the same.

The markets are nevertheless different. So the problem is to charge the creative people with the task of communicating the trucks' differences, especially in terms of whatever creative ideas are used. This task involves the way the point-of-sale is put together, the way the sales force is trained, the ways devised to communicate with fleet buyers, and the ways devised to communicate with owner-operators. How will IH have the dealer show the two trucks? How will the dealer demonstrate them? The differences have to be visible because, after all, they *are* in the units themselves.

To complicate the task—like trying to show two top-of-the-line Cadillac models, each to its own advantage for the customer—the same dealer, curiously, shows and "sells" both trucks. Fleet sales are generally done through the dealer organization, which takes a lower markup. The owner-operator, on the other hand, customarily comes to the dealership to view both trucks, and the dealer usually has both on hand.

The promotional creative technique started out with placing the truck in its competitive position, positioning the truck: "Here is the International truck, number one by any measure—the fleet version. The biggest selling truck with features not found on any other like-vehicle." The owner-operated technique was dealt with more simply, a competitive statement that simply said "CLASS" . . . number one in its own category. It was positioned differently, the literature looked different, the communication (copy) was different, the elements of composition were different, the point-of-sale approach was different. And the features were sold differently; the features highlighted in one group were different from those highlighted in the other.

For the 9670, presentations by both the advertising agency and the marketing services agency endeavored to show how the two different trucks would be handled. As it turned out, IH rejected the media recommendation, preferred and used the nonmedia positioning for the product, and selected this positioning as central to the media message.

It was the marketing services agency's view that the advertising agency had not affected an adequate separation between the fleet vehicle and the owner-operator vehicle. The advertising agency accepted the other agency's positioning and developed the advertising from it, including the corresponding creative development.

This is not always the case when two kinds of agencies work separately, but it happened with the 9670. And this is not a negative reflection on the advertising agency. But logic tells us that the marketing services agency had a better chance of being correct because of its greater involvement in the distribution channels. It knows more about the IH business—its dealer organization, its customers, its distribution channels—than does the advertising agency which, by the very nature of its activity, does not need to involve itself in the human media.

In order to perform a satisfactory service, the marketing services agency *must* know more than the advertising agency about the client's way of doing business. The business of the advertising agency is to know more than the marketing services agency does about the precise media that IH must use to communicate to the consumer. There is very little necessity, if any, for the advertising agency to be involved in the problems of the distribution channels.

The experience with IH's 9670 is a classic case of the rightness of the relationships that exist between the client and the two different agencies. Sales promotion is an organized marketing activity that influences *all* the people involved in the sale of a product or service into predictable action.

If it is discovered that any influence does not lead to a predictable action—that is, if the action is either enhanced or obstructed from what it should be—the marketing services agency and the client want to know, *must* know, where and why. This knowledge is the key to what is going to happen, or what might happen, on the next promotion. That is why long-term relationships are so important. In a long-term relationship, an agent gets to know the personality of the client company and develops a sense for what can and cannot be done.

The way this relates to the creative aspect of promotion is clear and important because advertising creativity and promotion creativity are very different. Creativity in advertising occurs within a given and fixed environment. For a 30-second or a 60-second TV or radio commercial, it is necessary to work within those time limits, and either medium's advantages or disadvantages are well-known by advertising's creative people. Marketers know what the medium is and they work to maximize its possibilities. In print, management must deal with a 9″ × 12″, or 8″ × 10″, or 8″ × 11″ format and accommodate the creative ideas to a fixed dimension.

Promotion creativity is concerned largely with *creating the medium*. Marketers create a piece for point-of-sale or perhaps an audio or video tool. Such creativity, for example, was accomplished in introducing the S-Series Trucks for International Harvester. The IH salespeople are well-known for being specification-minded. They are anxious to be in the enviable position of specifying the right truck for the customer: "We can spec the truck that's right for you!" And they deal only secondarily with trucks' general features and benefits for the average user.

Knowing this about IH salespeople, the marketing services agency's creative people decided, among other things, that they would make the *truck* the medium. Was this either broadcast media or print media? No. But it *was* the appropriate medium. The customer opened the door to the truck, and a tape went into a player and told the truck's story. When the door was closed, the tape rewound and set itself for the next playing.

The creative people, then, cannot be people who are specializing solely in one or two devices that the agency might wish to "push" in one year. Rather, they must be sufficiently versatile to implement whatever might be needed to further the effectiveness of a creative idea.

Once a medium is tentatively accepted, once concept, copy, and art have been created, the creative people submit the proposed promotion to a checklist of questions whose answers must meet client and agency acceptance:

CONCEPTS

1. How does this promotional tactic meet the marketing objective and strategy set by the client?
2. Is the promotion in keeping with the client's image and creative strategy? Is it reinforcing both?
3. Why is this promotion motivating to the consumer? Why is it motivating to the trade?
4. Is the promotion easy to communicate?
5. Does this promotion make sense for the period during which it will run? Is there enough time to plan and execute the promotion to meet the target date?
6. Are the resources and materials required—premiums or printing, for example—available from suppliers, and can they be delivered on time?
7. How would the promotion be executed? Have we thought out all the mechanics in order to identify problems and determine the best way to run the promotion?
8. Is the promotion affordable in the context of the budget? Is it sensible compared with other avenues of action?
9. Are there any attitudinal road blocks from the client's point of view?
10. What will be the presentation format?

Execution: Copy

1. What is the communications objective in the client's mind? What are we trying to accomplish? What are we trying to say and to whom are we trying to say it? What do we want them to do?
2. What is the overall progression of the copy? What is the logic of its organization? How does the story or message flow, and why does it flow that way?
3. What are the key messages, and how do headlines and copy bring them to the foreground of the communication?
4. Is the information presented factually correct? Is the copy

stylistically correct considering the brand's image and the target audience?

5. Does the copy conform to the client's creative guidelines in its use of brand names, trade or service marks, and advertising slogans?

6. Is the story effectively told? Is the message clearly communicated?

7. Is what has been written the best approach?

Execution: Art

1. What is the overall progression of the layout? What is the logic of its organization? How and why does the story or message flow?

2. Does the layout and selection of type give proper emphasis to the key messages?

3. What is the rationale for the choice of colors?

4. How do visuals reinforce or amplify the copy?

5. Are the visuals intended to be art or photography in the finished piece? What are the style considerations with either one?

6. What are the mechanics of the design? What is the intention of the design? How does it contribute to communication? Does the design mean additional time or cost requirements (die-cut, perforation, fold, score, special stock, etc.)? Why these choices?

7. Why have we settled on these elements, and what is the purpose of each?

8. What are the actual dimensions of the pieces? Is the layout being shown half-size, full-size, or twice size?

9. Are there any special things to know (fifth color, thermography, foils, plastics)? What is the background of the technology?

10. Is the story effectively told? Is the message clearly communicated?

11. Why is this the best way to go?

CHAPTER 9

Distribution and Fulfillment

The distribution and fulfillment function might seem extremely obvious in a promotion's scheme of things. Too frequently, however, not enough thought is given to this function until the very last moment.

All you need to fail is a "Match-the-Display" promotion advertised in freestanding inserts and magazines and no displays available to the retailer; or a game promotion advertised heavily on television and not enough game pieces to use in the stores; or a premium offered on a package back, and, when you try to replenish your inventory, a supplier who has gone out of business.

These may be remote possibilities, perhaps, but they make distribution and fulfillment very important ingredients for the success of any promotion or merchandising activity. Some years ago, an agency involved in the development of a merchandising display program for a packaged goods client created a unique point-of-sale piece that encouraged significant off-shelf display. There was a problem, however: the display unit itself was unusually bulky. The agency anticipated this bulk and was able to have the display packed one unit per carton. The program had been developed with the brand group and with the full knowledge and cooperation of the sales department.

The specifications were written and then submitted to the purchasing department to cut the final purchase order. When the purchasing department noted that the display was packed one unit to a carton, it became quite concerned. At that time corporate management policy stipulated that all point-of-sale material for distribution to the sales force be packed five display units to a carton. After a great deal of discussion about the inadvisability of packing these displays in that fashion, the rules of the purchasing department finally prevailed. The agency was advised by the brand group that this display was to be packed five displays per carton no matter what the consequences.

Any reasonable person by that time would have anticipated the ensuing problem. The agency ordered the displays packed as requested and wound up with a carton the size of an executive desk. Because the agency insisted on submitting carton size to its clients prior to delivery, it made this carton available to the brand group and the sales department along with a statement of compliance with the purchasing department's specifications. It also requested that those specifications be waived. Were it to ship that material as required, there would have been no way to fit the carton into the trunk of a sales representative's car, and it was from that trunk that the displays were to be distributed.

Reason finally prevailed, and the appropriate packing arrangements were made, the displays were shipped, and the promotion was successful.

Recently, a company offered a booklet and some product information to prospective customers via a freestanding insert in major newspaper ads around the country. Promotion personnel judged that they had done a reasonable job of anticipating the rate of response and had budgeted for 800,000 responses. Their projections were very close to what actually happened: they generated about 900,000 responses. That was close enough and nothing unusual occurred except that their return postage budget allowed for a 1½-ounce package. In the final production, however, the package to be mailed weighed 4 ounces. This meant that the postage budget, third class, would have to be more than doubled, thus throwing off the entire budget.

What had happened? The printer who had agreed to produce the booklet based on the original specifications discovered that he had significantly underordered his paper requirements, and he needed to substitute another stock to fill the order. Without informing his client, he went from a 40-pound stock, on which the mailing was based, to a 60-pound stock.

To compound the problem further, the sales department, in its peculiar wisdom, determined that the insertion of an extra piece of product literature would enhance the package, and it made this insertion adjustment without the full knowledge of the people responsible for the mailing.

What naturally occurred was a sort of a good news/bad news promotion. The good news was that the redemption rates were very close to the original projection, about 10 percent ahead; but the bad news was that the package that ultimately went to the field was not controlled, and the redemption budget was seriously compromised as a result.

Another company recently purchased a premium to offer on-pack for $1 and proof of purchase. It had been able to purchase 60,000 of these premiums for a very favorable price from a premium supplier-manufacturer with whom it had never done business before. Another good news/bad news situation arose: the company received many more requests than anticipated, but the supplier went out of business. The premium was a close-out and could not be duplicated. The ensuing problem of trying to get an acceptable substitute was a wrenching one.

Such examples of problems with distribution and fulfillment help illustrate that the best plan supported by the most creative idea with the biggest budget can fail if the material to be distributed is not in the field in a timely fashion, or if the necessary tools for the sales force and the trade are not usable, or if the materials are inadequate in any way. The very *best* promotion can be doomed to failure.

Fulfillment, then, is the ability of marketers to respond to specific requests from their own customers or consumers.

As a corollary, *distribution needs must be fulfilled with timeliness, convenience, and usability.*

We have all heard horror stories about displays that cannot be assembled in the field, thus reducing distribution cost-effectiveness. If an item is so fragile that it must be meticulously hand-packed, if packing costs go far beyond projected estimates, or if the package is so heavy that it must be handled on a flat-bed truck, the company will face distribution problems.

Careful attention must be paid to the problems of distribution and fulfillment, especially in the creative phase of a promotion when you are thinking about fulfilling the needs of the people in the field.

CHAPTER 10

Tools and Incentives

A promotion requires two important actions on the part of the client company. The company should seek to understand precisely what all those involved do to influence the sale of its product(s) or service(s) and to get the predictable action by the consumer; and it should arrange to prepare the tools that are useful to those people in the execution of their tasks.

What does the distributor actually do? What do the distributor salespeople actually do? What does the trade actually do? If the appropriate tool has to be a film, then the company should produce a film. If it has to be a flip chart, or a slide presentation, or a piece of literature, or an order form, then that is what should be prepared. The tool can indeed be as simple as an order form or a telephone message script if that is precisely what should be used to help make a sale.

The company must understand what the problems are for each individual in the distribution chain. If it produced a 45-minute videotape that related the company's entire story and product information better than anything that had ever been done, but if the food chain buyer had only four minutes to give to the sales representative, the videotape would be absolutely useless, an expensive, worthless tool. "You know what you can do with that tape. I've got four minutes, so put down on that form all the cogent information you can give me, and then get out. I've got 10 more people out there waiting to see me."

That is why the marketing department staff cannot sit in the office, without understanding the field activities, and recommend a bunch of sales tools that are not organized to coincide with how the sales force must operate in the real world. Such a kit is useless, absolutely useless. If there are no clearly demonstrable ways recommended to use the sales tools, and no reasons or ideas for their use, then a kit that simply offers an array of radio commercials, ad mats, halftone cuts, and point-of-sale materials represents, in all likelihood, money wasted and opportunities lost.

Such a kit should instead include example promotions utilizing certain tools under certain circumstances: "Here is our product line, and here are the tools in support of the product line. Here are the different ways you can decorate your store; here are the tools to run effective ads; here is what you can do with your sales force; here is what you can do with the kids in the neighborhood; here is what you can do with the schools; here is what you can do with the Chamber of Commerce, the PTA, and the other stores in the area." The kit should provide ideas that help the retailer promote and sell your products.

The day of simply presenting products for sale is over; that is what created a parity situation. The company must differentiate its product from all others. Its sales force, as well as its advertising, must make the trade receptive; it must deliver something to the distributor and retailer that is more than what the competition is delivering. What is the company doing for the customer that the competition is not? What kind of services does the company have that are different from those of the competition? How good is the company's co-op allowance? Can each salesperson positively answer this question: Am I helping the retailers run their businesses and make a profit?

CHAPTER 11

Execution: Telling People What Is Expected of Them

Good execution is a function of good communication. Yet communication is probably the single most frequently deficient ingredient in the whole promotion mix and often the most difficult to affect. Execution refers to people understanding and committing themselves to their roles in a promotional or merchandising program.

Experience tells us that if someone understands what he is supposed to do, he will do it much better and find it much easier to accomplish. This observation seems so self-evident that it should not even need to be mentioned. Yet, frequently, a marketing department develops an idea, executes it, then drops it into the hands of the sales department without supplying adequate information or assistance. Under such circumstances, which occur often, the sales department tends to be resistant and uncooperative. In this case, two autonomous entities exhibit a natural adversarial relationship toward one another:

Sales department: The marketing execs sit in their secure ivory tower and don't know what we face in the field.

Marketing department: Those sales reps always take the course of least resistance.

Sales department: The easiest way to get the sale is to do this [whatever tactic] and, therefore, I am going to do it.

Marketing department: Dammit, I am the marketing exec, and I say such-and-such; therefore, you, Mr. Salesperson, should respond accordingly.

Sales department: If I understood what you are saying, I would be able to help you get to the end you want. But no one can deal with anybody with a dammit-therefore-you-will attitude.

From their respective vantage points, all statements have a ring of authenticity. Marketing people do not stay in touch with the changes and dynamics of the marketplace. Salespeople typically take the course of least resistance because all they're asked to do is to make sales. There must be someone or something that interfaces with these two disciplines and functions to ensure that the objectives of the marketing department are achieved through the sales department. The only way to accomplish this is to blend the abilities and insights of each group into the actions of the other.

As pointed out in Chapter 5, one of the major roles of promotion is to function as a catalyst between the marketing department and the sales department. Promotion readily and regularly monitors the needs of the sales department and tries to provide salespeople with the tools to do their job.

Involvement, understanding, and experience are important catalysts. And, more than anything else, those involved must be willing to listen and understand that the sales force is not there to thwart the marketing department, and that the marketing department is not there to compel the sales force to do anything that it is not supposed to.

This leads us again to our definition of sales promotion and the predictable action. If a marketing person puts out a program and gives it to the sales force, but the sales representatives do not understand it, the marketer will indeed get a predictable action. Only this time, it will be a predictable nothing.

A case in point is a marketing services agency's experience

with the International Scout, International Harvester's four-wheel-drive vehicle. When IH had its Scout Division, the company found that bringing people into a Scout dealership was very difficult. In the first place, the company had to find a very selective market, people who were interested in off-road four-wheel vehicles. Secondly, in the Chicago market, for example, there were three IH dealerships, whereas there were 40 Ford dealerships, 30 Chevrolet dealerships, and numerous Chrysler dealerships. Three dealerships, therefore, represented a very small dealer structure in the face of competition, not to mention that they were located in remote suburban or industrial locations, clearly off the beaten path.

Efforts to get people into the IH dealership were not very successful. For years, IH had used things like sleeping bags and sports-related premiums as traffic incentives; and so the dealerships gave away quite a few sleeping bags. Moms came in just to get free sleeping bags for the kids.

Faced with the problem of getting *qualified* leads into the dealerships, IH asked its marketing services agency to develop a meaningful premium program. The basic idea of using a premium as a traffic incentive was perfectly all right, but what premium? With the cooperation of Rand-McNally, the agency developed a *North American Trail Guide,* which had a $7 value (see Figure 11–1). It felt that the *Guide* was directed specifically to people who would want to use the offer with off-road vehicles. Mom would not, in all likelihood, want a *Guide* nor would her kids; but, the agency reasoned, somebody who was interested in camping, hiking, and four-wheel-drive trailing vehicles would certainly want it.

Did the idea work? The premium served IH very well, and dealerships did get qualified leads for the Scout. But the promotion was not universally successful. In fact, in terms of regional success, it performed contrary to the company's expectations. In the state of New York, for example, the promotion was a big success, yet it failed in Colorado—one region where it should have succeeded.

Shortly thereafter, the marketing services agency went into the field to try to discover what had happened. In the successful regions, the regional managers examined the program, announced that it had great possibilities, and made it their business to get their personnel's full support for the pro-

FIGURE 11–1

North American Trail Guide **for International Harvester Scout Promotion**

Courtesy of International Harvester Company

motion: "Here is the scheduling, here is how we are going to use the displays, and here are the newspaper ads." Regional managers were fully cognizant of the importance of the support materials. They knew how and when to use them, and they knew that they had to let the public know what their dealerships were offering.

In the other regions, the regional management announced, in effect: "Here's another program from corporate headquarters. Set it up if you want." There was no leadership encouraging staff to get involved and, *in fact*, everyone was *not* involved as he should have been. As an agency spokesperson said later, "Unless you get everybody on board singing the same song, forget it in our business. You've got to make sure that top management [i.e., top regional management] is involved and doing what they should do."

Months and months of work were required to put together a

national atlas of all the wonderful country to trail-ride through. The atlas, a thick book with marvelous pictures, represented a large outlay of promotion money. It was the ideal premium; it related directly to the product.

How could this program be so successful in New York City, of all places, and yet fail miserably in places like Colorado, Wyoming, and Montana? The answer, discovered eventually, was simple: the problem lay in the communication—or the lack of it. In some dealerships boxes of trail guides were found packed under tables six months after the promotion was over. When asked about the unused *Guides,* one dealer replied, "Oh, I don't know. It was some stuff sent from corporate headquarters. I don't even know what it is. It's been sitting there six or eight months."

The ironic truth is that the marketing services agency, being an ostensible outsider, cannot *order* personnel to support the promotion. But management must do so if it is provided with the proper tools. In the unsuccessful regions, there was no communication from the regional managers to their own salespeople and ultimately to the dealers. They did not understand the promotion because they did not take the time to understand it. In fact, they did not even know how to think about it.

The regional manager of the New York market loved it. He got behind it, read all the communications, critically examined the *Guide,* and announced that this was an exciting idea. "That's right where our vehicles fit in. We are going to get really qualified test drivers. People who are interested in our book are by definition interested in our vehicles. It's going to be terrific, so let's support it and let's get our dealers to support it." He got the sales force all charged up, they encouraged dealers to run advertising, and they were successful.

What this qualified kind of success said to the marketing services agency and to IH management was that they had to do other things to ensure that the appropriate managers got behind a promotion. They could create an incentive program behind the promotion. They could make one-on-one presentations to each of the regional managers to communicate the importance of the idea and how effective it could be. Or they could simply have the most important person at corporate headquarters make a phone call to each of the regional managers.

If a company has the historical problem of salespeople not talking to marketing people, then a promotion must be well-planned and given extra impetus. If there is a deficiency in that promotion, the marketing department should work with regional management to identify that deficiency. If regional salespeople say, "We know what the realities are, and the marketing department can't tell us how to sell because we know more about that than they do," marketing people may respond by saying, "That's right, you *do* know more than we do, but we can *help* you sell and be sympathetic to your problems, so why don't we work together?"

What is the position of the marketing services agency in regard to such interdepartmental struggles? Is it up to the agency to make sure the marketing department communicates to those people in the field who might represent problem areas? Yes, it is part of the agency's function. An agency regularly provides its clients with communications that solve or anticipate these kinds of problems. Question-and-answer formats seem to work best: "Here is the kind of question the dealer might ask and here is the kind of answer you might think about giving him," "here is how to make it happen."

The fact that marketing people don't interact with sales people is a typical problem in some corporations. If whatever communications the agency prepares are left entirely in the hands of second-string or third-string personnel, there is hardly any way to gain predictable action, hardly any way to predict whether salespeople will be enthusiastic about a promotion.

Since promotion (and by extension promotion people) is the catalyst between the marketing and sales departments, should there be, and are there, specific talents or skills among the sales promotion people that are crucial to solving communication problems? The answer, of course, is yes. Promotion people cannot be just production people; they cannot be just salespeople; they cannot be just marketing people. Rather, they must be very sensitive to and experienced in the problems of both the marketing and the sales departments. They must be the broadest generalists available.

In many companies sales promotion is a thankless job. Sales promotion people are frequently identified as the people who execute the instructions of the brand group. They are reputed to be insensitive to either marketing *or* sales prob-lems; they create things—a coupon, a display—rather than get involved in the whole.

The deficiency lies not so much within the promotion per-son as within management's understanding of the role. To many organizations that stress the marketing, advertising, and sales departments, the sales promotion department is the also-ran, the afterthought. The image of the typical pro-motion person—an idea that is gradually disappearing—is one of an individual who knows the printer down the street, who can write a headline if called on to do so, or who can create a *thing*. The prototypical promotion person has an ar-ray of suppliers he can contact to supply premiums or sell the exhibits; but the promotion executive is not looked on with the same credibility, is not considered to have the same cre-dentials, as heads of the other departments.

All this is beginning to change. The experienced, sensitive, knowledgeable generalist is the person being sought more and more; it is this individual who is now being paid a large salary, and who is often being given a vice presidency. The ideal promotion person is one who can affect communications between departments that have objectives to meet, who un-derstands the needs of each group. Ideally this person should have the authority to seek and get input from each group. If he does not have delegated authority but is, instead, rele-gated to a position of executor, executing what management wants while relaying objectives to the sales department, then this firm's sales promotion formula, in all probability, relies on some other nontraditional communications link. In many corporate environments, the salespeople are the most misun-derstood and underrated. Increasing their effectiveness is of the utmost importance, and this means communicating with all those in the distribution chain—sales management, sales force, distributor principals, distributor salespeople, retailer, retail salespeople—whose cooperative spirit will help the company communicate with the consumer.

Retail salespeople include all those who work behind count-ers contacting the public directly. If a promotion consists of handing out game pieces for games conducted by fast food chains, then the entire distribution chain must depend on the person giving out pieces to each customer who purchases food. That customer cannot play without that piece. So it is absolutely necessary to impress on counter employees how important they are to the whole. They must be convinced how important their roles are in the success of the promotion.

An excellent example of involvement occurred recently on the local level (i.e., without the participation of any large promotional program on either a regional or national level). It involved a camera store in a medium-sized town in the Midwest. The camera store owner knew the owner of the local McDonald's franchise, and he asked if the McDonald's owner would be willing to participate in a small promotion that would build traffic in the camera store for film and photographic supplies. They arrived at a plan that was quite simple: in the local paper the camera store would run a small, continuing advertisement that was part coupon. If the consumer presented the coupon and brought in one roll of film to be developed, he would be given another coupon for a free regular-sized order of french fries. The offer was good at any of the McDonald's restaurants in the neighboring communities as well; all were owned by the same man. As a double incentive, the price of the developed film was reduced to approximately half its regular price at any of the local 24-hour film developers. When consumers picked up their film, they found the french fries coupon attached to the package. The coupon represented a 30-cent (at cost) premium. The camera store owner made an arrangement with a local film laboratory to develop the film instead of sending it to his standard supplier who was located over 60 miles away.

It is understandable that the low developing price would generate a high volume of business; but the actual response was far beyond what the camera store owner had anticipated. To his amazement, the consumer response was limited only by the availability of the french fry coupon; virtually *all* the coupons turned up at McDonald's and became a healthy traffic-builder there, too. The camera store traffic in film developing became so heavy that, after awhile, the owner did not care whether or not the consumer brought in the newspaper ad.

The key to this promotion is the fact that it was easy—easy to do, easy to understand. In addition to being an incentive, it was also a reminder. Consumers were going to take their film to that big impersonal drug store for processing, so why not instead take it to someone they knew? The coupon was good for something that consumers were purchasing all the time, as well.

The retailer was creating a strong sense of involvement, the consumer indeed became involved, and everyone won. The promotion was obviously worth more than 30 cents per customer.

Late in 1975, Indiana University's basketball team, on its way to a national championship, was playing a mismatched game in Bloomington, Indiana, with a small college. With two minutes to play, Indiana was leading 92 to 47. The crowd suddenly started chanting, "Defense! Defense! Defense!" An outsider could not imagine what was going on. None of this made any sense because the Indiana players could have laid down on the floor for the next two minutes each time the opposing team had the ball, and still they would have won. It did not make sense because he *was* an outsider and did not know that the local McDonald's franchise had made the offer to the crowd that could at any moment become a reality: if Indiana held its opponent to 50 points or fewer, every ticket holder at the game could present his ticket stub to McDonald's for a free hamburger. Not only was the crowd involved in the game, it was also involved with McDonald's; and everyone wanted that hamburger. And the fans went crazy. That is involvement of the first magnitude.

Good promotion execution then is a result of good communication, appropriate motivation, uncomplicated execution, and involvement by both internal and external publics.

CHAPTER 12

Evaluation: What Has Been Accomplished

It is no sin to fail. In fact if you are trying new promotion concepts you will occasionally fail. However, it is a *sin* to fail and not learn from it. That is why promotion evaluation is so important.

The client-company must ultimately ask itself how well the promotion worked.

Did we accomplish what we set out to do?

Was the strategy right?

Was the idea workable?

Was the production appropriate?

Did we spend too much or too little?

Did everyone understand what was expected of him?

Did the promotion work? If not, why not? If so, why?

The company will then know what its promotional capabilities are, and its marketing services or promotion agency can begin to build a body of knowledge about the company and about its market. Both will then have a better idea about future action and about all the steps necessary to produce a successful promotion. In the example of the stamp company, its marketing services agency in the future will not do anything or recommend anything to the company unless it is absolutely certain that the sales force can execute it. The agency could have said, "Well, the idea was bad, and the promotion did not work because of the bad idea." But that was not true. The idea was a good one. The agency that conducted the promotion for the International Harvester Scout could have said that the basic idea was a bad one because it worked in only 50 percent of the regions. That would have been a false deduction (and a bad analysis, as well).

You cannot simply look at the results and say, yes, it was good or, no, it was bad. Results can be great, yet the evaluation can be disappointing. If the results are impressive but no one really understood the promotion, you can imagine how much better the results could have been had everyone understood.

An evaluation, of course, should include a look at sales figures. A promotion, by definition, will create a sales peak. A good sales analysis will not establish a new base period at the peak. However, the *postpromotion* period will establish a new higher base if the promotion was successful—increasing sales to a level somewhere between the peak and the old base. The new level would be higher but not artificially so. To accept the peak level as the new base would be to make the same mistake the TV manufacturer made when it loaded up the trade during the year's first half (Chapter 7) only to discover that sales fell drastically when the trade could not accept any more new product.

Before any promotion begins there should be clear-cut agreement on its objectives and how the results of the promotion will be measured. Is the promotion designed to get incremental sales, new distribution, more flavors with existing customers, better trained salespeople, or a combination of all of these and more? As you can see, if the objective is training salespeople, new distribution will not provide an accurate measure of the stated objective.

Part III

Promotion Tactics

CHAPTER 13

An Overview

Once the objectives and strategies have been determined for a given program, the next and perhaps most creative task is to develop the appropriate tactic. Client companies frequently maintain that they are always looking for the big idea. Yet no one is quite certain what that big idea is. What a client is actually saying when he says, "Give me that big idea," is that the tactics he has used to date are now uninteresting and boring, and they do not motivate the people who have to execute a promotion idea.

And there, in a word, is the most important component of good promotion—*execution.*

Any number of situations could be cited where the tactical recommendations were breakthroughs. They concept-tested very well, they were unique in their construction, and were clearly different from other programs run by that company. There have been situations where successful concepts in Industry A failed miserably in Industry B. The explanation is, of course, that Industry A either had the people power, the systems, or the understanding to execute a given promotion concept, whereas Industry B did not.

The first screen any promotion tactic must be put through is the execution screen. No matter how new, innovative, creative, exciting, or energetic an idea may seem, if there is any question about the potential of the promoting company to execute it, a giant red flag of warning should be raised.

If there are situations that block a promoting company's ability to execute a tactic successfully, that idea must be disregarded. It should be the first order of business. However, just because some factor may hinder successful execution doesn't mean that the idea cannot be fulfilled in the long run. Successful execution may depend simply on providing better training or appropriate tools. It may depend on good selling borne of understanding. All issues that appear to block success must be examined and corrected, or the idea will have to be scrapped.

The second most important issue for successful execution of a promotion tactic is the ability to communicate the idea. If there are no reasonable communication vehicles—i.e., advertising, point-of-sale, direct mail, direct mailing (one-to-one communication)—the idea must be disregarded. If there is no way to tell anybody that you have the greatest idea in the world, people won't beat a path to your door. Similarly, if you create an idea so complex that it defies quick interpretation, the idea has to be reevaluated and considered when a new tactic is recommended.

Sometimes a promotion is so complicated that no one takes advantage of it: "Buy two, try them for 30 days, and if you like the product, send in this coupon and we will send you another coupon so that you may get a third free. Or, if you buy two and send in this coupon and you don't like our product, we will refund the purchase price of one, provided that you furnish a register tape indicating the price per unit." The marketing manager of the company that conceived that plan thought it was absolutely fair and equitable for both the consumer and his customer.

His logic went something like this: "Well, if you buy two and you don't like our product, you're not stuck with the second because we will refund the money. Moreover, if you were satisfied with the product, you could, at the end of 30 days, send in the coupon together with the proof-of-purchase and you would get a free coupon in the mail good for another one." The product retailed for $1.29, so the free coupon was worthwhile. The product's usage cycle, however, was approximately three months, and, you guessed it, the deadline from the date the sale began was six months. Obviously, this was an unrealistic timetable.

Another client asked his marketing services agency to invent some totally new, never-before-seen premium ideas. Bored with all the ideas available through standard premium vendors, he wanted to offer the consumer a product that had never been seen before. Excited about such an assignment, the agency did indeed produce four totally new, never-before-seen ideas, but it was smart enough to test them first. They were targeted at mothers with children between the ages of 3 and 10, so everyone was convinced that they would be relatively easy to test. To ensure a valid reading from the test, which was a mall intercept technique, the agency included a previously used growth chart. The results were interesting. The unique, never-before-seen-or-perhaps-even-imagined ideas had to be explained in very complex detail. Consumers had absolutely no frame of reference to help them determine whether they even wanted these products. The concept test revealed that the growth chart was a significantly better offer than any of the new, remarkable, breakthrough ideas. That client chose the growth tape promotion. It was well-communicated, well-executed, and an unprecedented success.

If an idea cannot be quickly and simply communicated through the available communication channels, then it must be disregarded.

The third caveat to successful promotion is budget. The idea must be affordable. Some of the hidden traps to affordability lie in the areas of fulfillment and distribution. Once the tactic is identified for the promotion, accurate cost estimates must be made. Estimates should include packaging, handling, postage, freight, mold, and finishing costs. There are a thousand components that can disrupt pricing. If even well-identified costs are not affordable or cannot be passed on to the consumer, the idea must be scrapped. In one instance, an agency rejected a client-suggested premium *because* the premium had the potential for being successful at the price point the client had selected. Packaging, fulfillment services, postage, and in-bound freight costs had not been anticipated; their inclusion caused a doubling of the proposed cost to the client and created an inescapable dilemma: the more successful the client's product became, the more money he lost.

THE ANATOMY OF A PROMOTION

The McDonald Muppet Glass Promotion had all the components essential to a good promotion. First, it was timely and kept pace with consumer trends. At the time the Muppet movie was in development, the recommendation was made to create a tie-in promotion between the two companies. The Muppets were then a very hot property. Second, anticipation became an important strategy. A year and a half before the Muppet movie made its debut for the American consumer, McDonald's marketing services agency began negotiating promotion rights to the movie. The people at Hensen & Associates were interested in such a tie-in and expressed a willingness to examine its possibilities. Next, the agency and the client began the more mechanical evaluative steps. The task was to determine, through research, the appropriateness of a tie-in between McDonald's and the Muppets. Since McDonald's had its own cast of characters—the Hamburgler, Ronald McDonald, Capt. Crook, and Big Mac—there was a tentative concern that a tie-in with such well-known characters as the Muppets would somehow confuse consumers. Special focus groups were initiated to determine the impact one group of characters might have on the other. To all involved, these evaluations were gratifying. The focus groups concluded that the Muppets would have no negative effect. All felt that the two groups of characters were commercially compatible and that a tie-in promotion between McDonald's and the Muppets could take place comfortably.

The agency then had to decide what to do. They could build a game around the movie. The characters could be intertwined. There could be a sweepstakes, premiums, or movie theater discount tickets. There could be a promotion whereby people who saw the movie could use their theater stubs to get discounts.

Obviously, many different tactics could have been used, but the agency had to test to find out which idea was most viable for their sales- and traffic-building objectives. The tests, a series of mall intercepts, helped determine which tactic was most acceptable. Premiums became the most consumer-acceptable kind of tie-in for McDonald's and the Muppets.

But what kind of premiums should be used? Dolls, mugs, glasses, posters? The most valuable idea was the Muppet Glass—the Great Mupper Caper Drinking Glass (see Figure 13–1). Research indicated not only the right direction to take but also suggested that, if properly executed, this idea might be the largest promotion in McDonald's history.

Arrangements had to be negotiated with Hensen & Associates. At this point, McDonald's management and its legal department assumed a primary role in the negotiations. McDonald's, in fact, finalized all details to the ultimate satisfaction of all parties involved.[1]

FIGURE 13–1

Complete Set of the Muppet Caper Drinking Glass Promotion

Courtesy of McDonald's Corporation

All preliminary details were then in place, but one of the biggest problems was yet to be solved. With only 10 months between the agreements and the time of execution, there remained the task of finding an appropriate source for the glasses—55 million of them. The agency's creative people worked in conjunction with McDonald's purchasing department to find a supplier capable of producing enough glasses in time to meet the necessary delivery commitments.

Once the appropriate manufacturing contracts were signed by McDonald's and the supplier, the next problem was to retrieve the appropriate out-takes from the movie. These out-takes would represent the first major communication step.

All McDonald's markets have local advertising managers. They are responsible for monitoring media buys and communicating various promotion programs offered to McDonald's operators in local markets. Regional and district managers work with local advertising agencies in each of these key markets. Working together, the local agency and the local advertising manager evaluate the information presented to them and then make recommendations to the local operator co-op.

To facilitate the promotion process, the agency created a document known as the "Blue Book." The "Blue Book" contained all the rationale, both marketing and creative, for the recommendation of the glasses promotion, together with projected performance expectations which the agency research had led individual markets to anticipate. The communication also had samples of the point-of-sale material planned. It had copies of the storyboards of the appropriate TV commercials. It included some media guidelines as to the gross rating point levels that the local markets should try to maintain in support of the promotion. It had ordering guidelines for the premium so that each operator had some basis for making ordering decisions. Finally, when applicable, recommendations were made concerning possible impact on crew levels.

If a recommended promotion is expected to be well-supported by the corporation and the local markets, the agency frequently puts together an audio-visual presentation to be made at co-op meetings by the advertising managers and local advertising agencies. This could take the form of a scripted slide presentation or even a videotape employing the marketing management people in corporate headquarters.

With all this information, the local markets then made the decision whether to participate in the promotion. The decision to participate is traditionally made on an entire market basis as opposed to a store-by-store basis. After the presentation is made, the co-op votes either to participate and support the recommended promotion or to ignore it. If the majority vote is in favor of the promotion, it usually runs on a market-wide basis.

The projections on the Muppet glasses promotion were so strong that it was approved on a national basis, and the decision was made to run the promotion commercials on national network television. This, of course, meant that the advertising reach behind this promotion would be fairly substantial and would provide even greater media coverage than might otherwise be expected from just a locally supported promotion.

Up to this point, there was the right partnership, the right promotion idea, and unanimous participation. Added to all this were some exciting point-of-sale materials and some wonderfully creative TV commercials. All the ingredients of a successful promotion were present. Or were they?

There was still a missing ingredient. What do you want to happen at the store? What do you want the store manager to do? What do you want the crew kids to do now? To help instruct store managers in their roles in the promotion, the agency created a store manager's guide. With the help of Universal Studios' field marketing staff, McDonald's corporate headquarters, and some of the McDonald's field marketing personnel, the agency created an extensive manual of activities for the store manager. It contained suggested promotion ideas, ways to tie in with local theaters and department stores who carried licensed Muppet products, potential tie-in ideas with schools and art schools, and other ideas that could be executed at the store level to make the promotion more exciting and more stimulating to both customers and crew kids.

The role of the crew kids was crucial in executing the promotion properly. They had to know exactly how to react to any situation that might arise when customers were told that, instead of getting their choice of the four glasses, they had to settle for the glass that was available that week. That situation could obviously pose an occasional problem. Some folks might have wanted glasses A and B and wanted both of them during week C, but, by the time week C came along, glasses A and B were gone and glass D was not going to be available until the following week. The crew kids had to understand such complications and be able to address customers' requests. There was going to be breakage, as well, and planning ways to handle such problems was equally important. And, finally, among the most important guidelines for crew kids were their suggested selling techniques.

To meet these needs, the agency created a 13-minute tape which communicated to the crew kids, in very creative and clever ways, how to handle each of these three different situations and what, in fact, was expected of them during the term of the promotion.

Point-of-sale materials were prepared for each store, drawing consumers' attention to the promotion as soon as they walked in (see Figure 13–2). Among these was a very effective display piece indicating which glass was to be offered each week. This display enabled consumers to determine (without asking the crew) which glass was being featured for that week's distribution.

One of the important aspects of the display graphics was the quality of reproduction, especially for the Muppet characters, and that quality gave the McDonald's Corporation an unexpected benefit. Jim Hensen himself was so enthusiastic that he directed his company to order enough additional displays to be used in all of the theaters around the country during the introduction of the movie. Though the theater version of the display lacked the McDonald's identification, it nevertheless created an important continuity between the theaters and the individual McDonald's stores.

Subsidiary problems had to be anticipated and solved. Since the original research indicated that the promotion was going to be very successful, the operators were going to be involved in ordering substantial numbers of glasses. The logistics of this phase alone were sufficiently intimidating for everyone to consider canceling the entire promotion.

FIGURE 13-2

**McDonald's Muppet Caper Glass Promotion
Point-of-Purchase Kit**

Courtesy of McDonald's Corporation

McDonald's stores are organized to be the epitome of operating efficiency; and that tightly woven and efficient machine was simply not structured to accommodate thousands of cases of glasses. Arrangements had to be made so individual operators would have steady supplies of glasses without clogging up their storage facilities.

First, to alleviate this problem, shipments were scheduled to arrive at McDonald's distribution centers in a preplanned sequential pattern to prevent any center from being inundated in one day. Second, a distribution center *for* the distribution centers was organized to deliver the week's available glasses in a timely and convenient fashion to the stores.

Fortunately for all concerned, McDonald's distribution system is so meticulously managed by the corporation and the independent businesspeople who operate it that the company was able to devise a methodical way of accepting the product from the manufacturer and distributing it to the stores without the confusion intrinsic in such a large task.

The final step involved putting together the evaluation criteria. The backlog of accumulated research data compiled by the McDonald's research department was indispensable to this final phase. McDonald's has a base of data from mall intercepts on a variety of different promotion activities against which it can measure the effectiveness of any new promotional activities. When the agency had earlier compared the mall intercepts responses to the glasses promotion with this base line data, it concluded that it had a big winner.

McDonald's research department's method is to retrieve the data from mall intercepts, compare it to the base data that it has on the glasses promotion, and do a business projection against a number which it calls *expected volume.* The expected volume consists of the dollars and cents or transactions McDonald's Corporation would expect to achieve in the course of a given period by simply continuing to run "normal" levels of advertising and "normal" levels of promotion. The expected volume is the number that forms the base against which all promotions are measured. As a hypothetical example, if a corporation operates on the normally expected volume of a 5 percent increase in sales for the course of the year, it might determine that a promotion idea might deliver an additional 5 percent, or a cumulative 10 percent, above the previous year's promotion.

The evaluation criteria for the Muppets promotion were therefore set by this method: in fact, the promotion at that time was the most successful in McDonald's history.

MARKETING RATIONALE

What was the marketing rationale that led both the McDonald's marketing department and the marketing services agency down this path from the beginning? When a company must contend with continuity of image, it always faces the question of timing. What is the benefit of tying in with a Muppet movie at the end of June when kids are out of school and on vacation?

All those involved in the fast food business look for very

high energy promotions to kick off the summer season. Since the summer months are the highest volume months of the year, it is important to get into the key selling season with as much momentum as a company can generate. This promotion idea and the timing of the movie release coincided perfectly with the needs of McDonald's; and, of course, the Muppets have always had a broad appeal. At the height of their popularity, appealing to both children and adults, the Muppets had one of the highest-rated shows on television with perhaps the broadest audience, in demographic terms, of any show on the air at that time.

SUMMARY

The promotion of the McDonald's Great Muppet Caper thus began as any good promotion should. All those involved identified an opportunity and pursued it. Having established interest, they determined the compatibility of the two casts of characters, McDonald's and the Muppets. When they determined the tactic, offering a premium, they searched for the best possible premium for that promotion.

Communication was the next logical step. The operators in the field were informed of the promotion idea and were offered the opportunity to participate. Without them, this particular promotion would fail. The operators, in turn, responded enthusiastically and guaranteed their financial participation.

Adequate supplies of the drinking glasses and their timely and appropriate distribution then had to be ensured before McDonald's could carry out its next step—communication to store managers. Store managers had to be informed about all aspects of the promotion: availability of premiums, kinds of advertising planned (both broadcast and print), appropriate levels of advertising scheduled, kinds of point-of-sale material for in-store display, and guidelines for local tie-in promotions and advertising to help each individual operator. Proper execution at the store level meant in-store training materials for the crew kids (a videotape was used for this purpose).

Finally, evaluating the results of the work done on the promotion added to McDonald's bank of already-existing information for the next promotion.

CHAPTER 14

Couponing

Couponing is currently the most popular of all the promotion tactics. An estimated 160 billion coupons were distributed in 1984—most of them by freestanding inserts (FSI) in Sunday newspapers or in Best Food Day. These inserts are usually multibranded with multiple offers, and most syndicators attempt to give product exclusivity in each category.

Newspaper co-op programs also involve coupons, an idea that burst on the scene several years ago, though there are indications that the trend may be declining. The benefit to each sponsoring manufacturer is that the co-op, run-of-press (ROP) coupon provides some economies of a magnitude that an individual manufacturer could not otherwise enjoy. The newspaper page that is filled with coupons tends to be regularly shopped by the promotion-prone homemaker.

Newspapers, moreover, often prove to be an important tool to the manufacturer in specialized, regional promotions. Through the use of ROP newspaper couponing, the manufacturer may do some very selective, local and regional market-ing and promotion, especially where there are local distribu-tors or franchisees who represent the manufacturer in a given region. A current trend is for food brokers who repre-sent a multiple line of products to put together their own newspaper couponing program co-oped by all the represented manufacturers.

Other coupons appear in magazines such as *Family Circle, Woman's Day, TV Guide,* and *Reader's Digest.* These publica-tions do particularly well with the distribution of coupons and are, in fact, "shopped" with almost the same alacrity as freestanding inserts.

Other coupons are distributed via direct mail (e.g., the co-op direct mail packages of Carole Wright by Donnelly), or are sent to the consumer by local newspapers' ROP, or are availa-ble as in-ad coupons of the local retailer. The in-ad coupons run by retailers are usually paid for either in full or in part by the manufacturers whose products are featured.

There are, in addition, in-pack coupons, on-pack coupons torn off and used immediately at retail, and in-store coupons. The in-store variety obviously gets a great deal of redemption since it is frequently displayed with the product; people who buy the product tend to pick up the coupon.

Another couponing method is intercepts: people are inter-cepted and presented with coupons as they enter the retail store. This, too, has a high redemption rate. Electronic cou-pons are used successfully in the fast food industry. One ham-burger chain required consumers to repeat the chain's cur-rent advertising slogan in return for a discount on the prod-uct ordered.

In view of all this activity, the question arises, "Why so much couponing?" The answer is, of course, that the coupon is easy to execute. Manufacturers simply decide what media they wish to use to distribute the coupon, and all retailers around the country honor coupons with purchase. The re-tailers themselves are interested because they are able to col-lect the full face value *plus* a handling charge (from 7 to 10 cents per coupon accepted) from the sponsoring manufac-turer.

Why is it so easy to execute a coupon program? Simply be-cause no one is involved other than the cashier at retail.

Neither the sales force nor the retailers need to make any special effort, unless the retailers distribute their own coupons or a co-op coupon with the manufacturer. Even then store personnel are not usually involved. The obvious secret of couponing is that execution does not rely on any of the human media. The single major need is to convince retailers that the distribution of a coupon will enhance traffic and/or sales in their stores and, therefore, they should make a special feature of that product.

The key to the general acceptance of coupons as a promotion tool is that they provide retailers with an additional opportunity to use coupons to promote their own businesses. Retailers may frequently run promotions offering two and three times the coupon's value. If there were a 25 cent coupon for Tide detergent, for example, retailers might make it 50 cents or 75 cents. Sometimes the extra values are co-oped with the manufacturer. In most instances, however, multiples of coupons are the exclusive province of the retailer.

COUPONS AND THE CONSUMER

Nielsen Clearing House has just completed a study entitled "What Consumers Think of Coupons."[1] Coupon usage has mushroomed over the past decade as consumers continue to battle inflation and struggle to stretch the household dollar. The number of households using coupons increased to 71 percent in 1984, up from 58 percent in 1971. Contributing to the trend, according to Nielsen, is the use of coupons by manufacturers in varied product categories and innovative coupon distribution vehicles that help manufacturers deliver promotions more effectively and economically.

Coupon usage appears to be directly tied to household size—67 percent of households of one person and 87 percent of households of four or more persons use them. Even more dramatic is the increase of heavy users; most are concentrated in households of three or more members. The highest proportion of heavy users is also concentrated in the 31- to 45-year-old age bracket and among those who earn from $20,000 to $35,000 a year. The more a household spends on groceries each week, the more likely its shoppers are to be heavy coupon users.

There are racial distinctions among coupon users as well. White households are more likely to use coupons than black households, 81 percent to 72 percent. Seventy-four percent of Spanish-speaking households use coupons. Women use more coupons than men, 83 percent to 57 percent, and heavy users among women outnumber men almost two to one.

Many areas of the country are about equal in coupon usage. Some exceptions are the Southwest and the Pacific states where usage is very low. The proportion of heavy users is very high in the Northeast and the East Central states, representing nearly a third of all coupon users; only 13 percent of all coupon users live in the Pacific states. There is probably no readily available explanation for some of these discrepancies. One possible explanation might be that, in the East, Northeast, and East Central regions, there is more in-ad couponing and more double and triple values for coupons. These practices may cause a rise in usage. As for the lower response in the Southwest and Pacific states, there seems to be no easy answer.

Usage rates are also drawing categories outside of the normal food and household products—toiletry redemptions in 1975 were 73 percent, and in 1984, 88 percent. Drug product redemption in 1975 was 36 percent, and in 1984, 57 percent.

The study revealed numerous other respondent characteristics. About 50 percent always make out a shopping list before going to the store; another 18 percent usually do. But, more important to marketers, 60 percent always or usually refer to their coupons in preparing a shopping list. Face value of coupons is viewed differently by different people. Most consumers will use a lower-valued coupon to purchase their regular brand, while only a higher-valued coupon will induce them to try a new brand. Twenty-seven percent said that a 25-cent coupon might induce them, while 51 percent said that the coupon would have to be even higher than that.

Brand loyalty is still important among consumers; 86 percent claimed that they were loyal to certain brands. When asked what was needed to make them switch, 38 percent were ambivalent about the influence of coupons; only 6 percent would use them, while 28 percent said they would seriously consider a coupon if they felt that the product was comparable to what they currently use (indicating prima facie evidence of product parity again). Nearly two thirds said that an in- or on-pack coupon would influence them to repurchase a product, but only if they liked it, which affirms once more that there is no substitute for product quality.

But what if a coupon were not available in the store of the consumer's choice? Twenty-five percent would go to another store looking for the offer, 23 percent would purchase a different brand, 32 percent would postpone the purchase, and 12 percent would simply discard the coupon.

Current research, therefore, seems to indicate that coupons are an important economic tool for consumers. Respondents cited three basic reasons for using coupons: they save money, they reduce the cost of the products purchased, they tell consumers about products and encourage them to try new products.

REACTIONS TO COUPONS: CONSUMER, TRADE, MANUFACTURER

How do consumers feel about couponing? They love it, pure and simple. Thousands of American households use coupons. Homemakers bring their card cases of alphabetized coupons to the store. Some shoppers actually do all their shopping based on available coupons. Retailers often provide bins for shoppers to discard their unwanted coupons in exchange for others. Despite considerable product parity, despite advertising parity, the coupon is the great tie-breaker. (For examples of coupon promotions, see Figure 14–1.)

In addition to their ease of execution, coupons can be used very selectively, and their use can be timed so that manufacturers can control their promotion periods. The trade likes them because they require little else beyond accepting and forwarding them to clearing houses. Consumers like them because they help save money, and manufacturers like them because they are generally accepted as marketing-merchandising-promotion vehicles.

Manufacturers, on the other hand, must be careful not to fool themselves about the volume they get from couponing. In reality, the manufacturer may simply be rearranging selling patterns to accommodate the couponing. In fact, couponing may have an impact on production. It may have an impact on

FIGURE 14-1

Examples of Coupon Promotions

Courtesy of McCormick & Company, Inc.

Courtesy of Colgate-Palmolive Company

FIGURE 14-1 *(concluded)*

Courtesy of Gaines Foods, Inc.

Example of a Successful Coupon Promotion that Was Run by Kodak

Courtesy of Eastman Kodak Company

raw material supply. It may even be related to a multibrand company or broker distribution system where manufacturers know they will not get featured 32 weeks a year by the retailer, so they must pick and choose their spots in the retailer's promotion calendar.

Some brands handle their promotions on a historical basis. If they run a coupon in January of year 1, they run a coupon in January of year 2. Soon their couponing cycle becomes accepted *and* anticipated by the buyer at retail.

COUPON BUDGETING

Budgets are an important consideration when selecting the media for coupon distribution. Each medium enjoys a different redemption rate; and it is not axiomatic that the more you sell, the more you make. What may be true is that the more you sell on deal, the less you make. But if there is no deal, you may not be able to distribute all the products you manufacture.

For example, if manufacturers are convinced that a coupon is a good selling tool, but they don't want to absorb many redemption costs, they might decide to run the coupon in a Sunday supplement magazine. This is a medium where redemption rates have been declining in recent years, but it nevertheless provides a local flavor to the coupon which most retailers like. So manufacturers may limit their exposure but maximize their ability to sell against a Sunday supplement local market.

One note of caution about redemption rate statistics: while the A. C. Nielsen figures are accurate, they are only averages. And is difficult to build budgets based on average figures. Experience tells us that each category and each brand within that category will react differently to various media. Average response, for example, for direct mail delivered coupons is between 9 and 9½ percent. One well-known client company realizes a redemption rate of between 50 and 60 percent for a direct response coupon offer. Another company regularly gets from 10 to 12 percent redemption on freestanding inserts' delivered coupons where the media average is under 5 percent. The point is that average redemption rates by medium can be helpful, but each product category and each brand has its own redemption experience. Budgets, therefore, must be built on that experience rather than on media redemption averages.

DIRECT MAIL DISTRIBUTION OF COUPONS

Direct mail distribution of coupons is a highly selective method because its major benefit is to place the coupon directly in the hands of the consumer who is quickly involved with a specific coupon. Direct mail provides manufacturers with some notable opportunities. They can focus sharply on specific market areas—if they are handling their own coupon distribution, they can distribute by neighborhood, by section of a city, by ZIP Code, by census tract, or by demographically appealing area. In addition, there are systems where manufacturers can distribute coupons by specific streets.

High redemption rates are one of the most attractive benefits of direct mail couponing. Except for in-pack and on-pack couponing, direct mail couponing has the highest redemption rate response.[2]

Direct mail coupons are distributed with either solo mailings or co-op mailings. Solo mailings focus on specific trading areas and specific sales territories. Auto dealers, banks, savings and loans, furniture and appliance dealers, and hardware store operators all do solo mailings, but they tend to make their mailings multiproduct in nature. The obvious advantage to a solo mailing is that it can reach specific consumers. Co-op mailings demand a broad appeal with a wide array of products, such as health and beauty aids, food products, and grocery items. The most commonly known co-op mailing, Carole Wright mailings by Donnelly, can reach as many as 45 million households. A co-op mailing program precludes the kind of selectivity that can be achieved with solo mailings.

GROUP PROMOTIONS COUPONING

Group promotions means multiple brands (not one brand with multiple flavors or sizes) appearing in *one advertisement* (not in a direct response coupon co-op). Research conducted by Frankel and Company in 1984 indicated that brand recognition is lower when multiple brands are featured. Further, the redemption rates for a multiple brand coupon promotion are lower than they would be with simple, clear, easy-to-understand single coupon offers. Certain overlay promotions, sweepstakes, and contests also result in lower coupon redemption rates.

The reasons are clear. It is usually more difficult to communicate clearly in an advertisement that has to explain the intricacies of a tie-in promotion and, at the same time, provide the rules for contests and sweepstakes. The consumer is unlikely to invest the time necessary to understand the communication. Consequently, redemption rates are lower. Such conclusions, though, should not be confused with studies indicating that leadership goes up when sweepstakes and contests are included in a piece of brand advertising.

MAGAZINE COUPONING

Magazines feature two types of coupons: the on-page variety, and the tipped-in, pop-up, or fall-out variety. Those in the latter group generally get better than double the response of on-page coupons. The costs are significantly greater than those of on-page coupons and must be evaluated based on the experience of the individual brand. Pop-up, tipped-in, fall-out coupons may or may not be cost-effective.

Perhaps the most interesting aspect of magazine couponing compared with those of freestanding inserts, direct mail, and newspaper couponing is the extended length of term for a given coupon. The inconvenience of having coupons appear at retail 12 months after the magazine has been published is not unusual. Of course, strict adherence to expiration dates will avoid this problem.

IN-PACK OR ON-PACK COUPONING

Package-delivered in-pack (or on-pack) couponing, some of which is called cross-ruff couponing (or distributing for another brand or manufacturer) is known for its particularly high response rate. The in-pack coupon is used primarily as a reward to a consumer, and it naturally encourages and stimulates repeat purchase.

In-packs are frequently used for multiple brands with a common manufacturer. For example, a multibrand manufacturer might wish to include a whole series of coupons for one of its cereals, its coffee, its salad dressing mix, or its dessert powder.

IN-STORE COUPONING

The in-store (or at-the-store) coupon is delivered to consumers in the store, frequently in conjunction with some kind of product sampling; it is frequently used to intercept shoppers before they begin their regular shopping. Sampling and product demonstration with coupon activity usually generates quite a bit of case movement, and many stores like this just to create some energy at retail. This kind of in-store couponing is very expensive but very effective. Manufacturers often use these combined activities to improve relationships with a given chain.

COMPUTER/VIDEO IN-STORE COUPONING

Computer/video in-store couponing is a rather new area and method of coupon distribution that offers some exciting research opportunities. Since each consumer using the computer has an ID number and UPC product code coupons are dispensed, it is possible for the marketing community to identify the coupon and the redeemer.

Video couponing emerged several years ago with computer coupon dispensing in several Safeway stores in the Dallas market. Here is how the idea works: the shopper enters the shopping card number into a machine, and the computer reads the number much the same way an automatic teller machine at the bank identifies customers. The screen on the terminal then reveals a picture of the coupon available at that moment. The shopper simply touches the illustration for the desired coupons, and the terminal prints and dispenses the two coupons selected. A special security feature prevents the shopper from entering the card a second time for the same coupons.

The first firm to enter this market was Electronic Advertising Network. The Coupon Counter, a Massachusetts-based company that offers additional research information through what it calls its Cue-Cop Division, is introducing video coupons that will be tested in Chicago.

Catalina Marketing is working with Wegman's in Rochester, New York, to develop a system tied to scanner equipment. A unique feature of its program will allow competitive coupons to be dispensed once the checkout scanner identifies the purchase.

A NOTE ON CREATIVITY IN COUPONING

In the marketing and distribution of packaged goods products, both the consumer and the trade have come to accept the coupon as a way of life. And they prefer that a coupon look like a coupon. Too often designers get carried away with their efforts to decorate the coupon, and then both consumers and the trade have trouble trying to decipher its value. Research has established that the simpler and more direct the creative message, the greater the consumer response. With a clear product shot, one simple copy message and an easy-to-understand value, all on an obvious coupon, will out-pull promotion ads with complex messages and overly designed graphics whose coupons are either graphically hidden or minimized. In other words, simple and strong works much better than complicated and tricky.

MISREDEMPTION

Misredemption of manufacturers' coupons continues to be a problem. Misredemption is defined as any attempt to collect coupons, handling fees, and face values for a brand that the retailer has not actually purchased or sold. Examples of obvious situations are gang-cut coupons that have been obtained from printing overruns or coupons that have been cut from unsold or undelivered newspapers and magazines. One example cited in the *Sales Promotion Monitor* involved a store manager's wife who spent most of her days cutting out coupons for a product that neither she nor her husband had any intention of purchasing. The manager then submitted those coupons to the clearinghouse for reimbursement and handling fees.

The scope of the problem is estimated by some experts in the field to be as high as 20 percent of all coupons handled; others feel that even 20 percent may be a conservative number. Unfortunately, there are no bona fide data on the specifics of the problem, but considering that 160.2 billion coupons were distributed in 1984, the potential scope of the problem is apparent.

Coupon fraud is a crime; and since claims are submitted through the U.S. mail, mail fraud is a felony class federal offense. Thanks to the diligence of the U.S. Postal Service, however, and to the cooperation of industry components, mis-redemption is gradually being controlled.

CHAPTER 15

Rebates, Refunds, and Premiums

When the prospect of government price controls loomed over the automotive industry several years ago, the rebate/refund promotion tactic came of age.

The automotive industry then became understandably concerned that it would be blocked by the Federal Trade Commission from establishing any further price increases for the foreseeable future. To circumvent the problem, it raised automobile prices a disproportionate amount and then introduced the rebate as a method of adding legitimacy to pricing. This maneuver constituted the establishment of rebates and refunds as a viable promotion tool.

Today, even though the price freeze threat has lifted, the automotive and other industries still make aggressive use of the refund as their favorite promotion tool.

Donnelley Marketing, in its sixth annual survey of promotional practices, reveals that money-back offers and cash refunds declined slightly from 1981 to 1983. In 1981, 87 percent of people surveyed said that they had used refunds and rebates, whereas in 1983, only 83 percent had done so.

In that same period, couponing went from 95 to 93 percent. Couponing is by far the most popular promotion and viewed as the most important by marketers. Second place goes to cents-off promotions, and third place goes to money-back offers and cash refunds.

REASONS FOR POPULARITY

Probably the foremost reason for the popularity of refunds involves their ease of execution. Success or failure of a refund/rebate promotion does not rely on the trade or the sales force, unless all of the communication for the offer is done through point-of-sale. Manufacturers can advertise the offer, make the offer available in- or on-pack, hire a fulfillment house, and have a promotion off and running. On the other hand, if point-of-sale materials are required to communicate the program, then the trade becomes involved, and the process becomes a little more complicated.

Refund offers are communicated in essentially four ways: (1) through print media, (2) by point-of-sale, (3) in- and on-pack, and (4) with multimedia. The trends are interesting in that multimedia and point-of-sale enjoy the most growth in communicating refund offers.

Limited misredemption is another reason for the popularity of refunds. Because most proofs are clearly defined, the misredemption problem that exists with couponing is minimally troublesome.

MARKETING REASONS FOR REFUNDS

Refunds are used for a number of important marketing reasons. Companies in the automotive industry use refunds as a pricing mechanism in an effort, they feel, to remain competitive. In addition, there are several generic reasons. One is to induce trial. The money-back guarantee is frequently the key promotion idea in the introduction of a new product or a new size or, less frequently, a new package. A second is to induce multiple purchases where the consumer is encouraged to select more than one of a given product: "Buy one at $1.19 and/

or buy two at $1.19 each and get a $1 rebate." Another reason is to promote larger sizes, particularly those of detergent packages: "Buy the 48-ounce package at the regular price, or get the 64-ounce package at the regular price and we will refund the difference." This is also called "trading up," usually to larger sizes or to higher quality.

Loading the consumer is another reason for the refund: "If you buy three packages of XYZ rather than your normal one package, we'll send you a $2 rebate." This is a fairly common regional practice among soft drink companies. They like to load the consumer with product because they know that soft drinks, once in the home, tend to be consumed. They also know that, if the consumer is well-stocked with a particular brand of soft drink, he will be less likely to buy the competitive product.

Another inventive promotion idea involving a refund might be called "companion product." A multiple brand manufacturer will combine one of its high-velocity brands with a new product or a less frequently purchased product in the hope of inducing trial *and* velocity for the second product. Pepsi-Cola recently offered its two-liter Pepsi at a feature price alongside its new brand, Slice; if consumers bought both Pepsi and Slice, they could send their register tape to a redemption house and get $1 refund.

Sometimes the tie-in is not quite as direct. The Seven-Up Company has offered refunds on hamburger and produce. The twist here is that Seven-Up is then able to get off-shelf display. With the hamburger, Seven-Up used an off-shelf display in the meat section. For the purchase of two, two-liter bottles and a minimum of $2 worth of hamburger, the consumer could get a $2 refund from the Seven-Up Company with proof-of-purchase of the 7UP and the register tape. With the produce, Seven-Up used an off-shelf display of Diet 7UP with fresh fruit and vegetables.

The progressive refund concept is another tactic of some interest to the marketing community, although current examples are lacking. The basic idea is that, for one proof-of-purchase, consumers get a refund of 75 cents, for two they get $3, and for three they get, say, $6.

The refund as a promotion device has provoked some interest among marketers. Some manufacturers have offered a contest-type refund. This involves a coupon refund using a rub-and-win game card. The consumer sends the card to the manufacturer, who guarantees a minimum value for the refund coupon and offers a chance to win big prizes. Frankel and Company has trademarked a promotion concept called REFUNS™. The concept behind REFUNS™ is that, with the appropriate proof-of-purchase, the consumer gets a refund; the refund is the amount that appears under a rub-and-win certificate that is either mailed or included in a freestanding insert. The consumer gets a $1 refund at the minimum and has the potential for getting tens of thousands of dollars as a refund for complying with the purchase requirements of the base offer.

The refund-as-an-overlay is a promotion tactic of dubious worth, and Frankel and Company's "Stopping Power" Research in 1984 corroborates this assertion. This tactic tends to confuse advertising and communication. The strategy is something like this: "Well, if we have a coupon, and we offer a rebate on top of the coupon and maybe throw in a sweepstakes or a contest as well, all of these are good, workable, and viable tactics."

This strategy is wrong. More is less. Any consumer offer must stand the test of clarity, and there is little chance this strategy will be clear to most consumers. If a company is running a contest, a refund overlay added to it will usually disrupt the communication of the sweepstakes and will probably not make the benefits of the refund clear. Multiple tactics in any kind of communication, whether point-of-sale, direct mail, advertising, or whatever, tend to make any offer difficult for the consumer to understand and respond to.

Refunds in Coupons or Cash. A controversy is currently raging over the respective merits of refunds in the form of coupons or cash. For a long time, some contended that a cash refund out-pulled coupons or drafts; but recent Nielsen data suggests that coupon refunds, when offered at the point-of-sale or on-pack, actually out-pull cash, and they out-pull drafts in an in- or on-pack.

Supporters of the coupon refund cite other benefits. The coupon, they say, encourages repurchasing of the product, and that adds appeal to the trade when contrasted with cash, which can be spent anywhere. Both benefits, repurchase and trade appeal, enjoy no reduction in response and redemption rates. A third benefit ascribed to the coupon refund is its lack of slippage. About 85 to 90 percent of refund coupons are redeemed, representing a significant dollar volume—depending on the product, of course.

The principal negative aspect to refunds and rebates is the delayed reward for action. Even in the simplest, most direct refund, where there is only one proof required, the consumer must take some inordinate action to get the reward. And that reward is delayed rather than being an instant benefit at the point-of-sale. The consumer must make the purchase, submit the appropriate evidence of purchase, and then wait.

Among the many fine surveys conducted and published by A. C. Nielsen, one concerns the factors that influence refund response rates. These data provide insight into planning a refund offer. Important considerations involve the method of distribution, the number and types of proof-of-purchase required, the value of the refund offer, and the refund's value relative to product price. Further considerations should address such issues as number of choices offered, duration of the promotion, design appeal of offer and advertisement, size of the brand's consumer franchise and retail availability, proper promotion controls, advertisement and publicity with regard to media selection (i.e., refund columns or magazines).

Budgeting of refund promotions must also be considered. There is the cost of fulfillment services, the cost of check printing, the cost of return postage, and the cost of the media involved in communicating the offer. If the refund is a coupon refund, there are printing and distribution costs.

As with most tactics, the details involved in the implementation of rebates and refunds can make or break a promotion.

PREMIUMS

A premium is generally defined as an article of merchandise delivered to a target audience as an added value and, therefore, as an incentive to action. A premium may be directed to consumers of a product to encourage them to purchase it or to visit a store; it may be directed toward sellers of a product to motivate them to perform a specified action.

A premium can move, motivate, stimulate, and excite people. It's the string attached to the action you want performed.

In-/On-Pack Premiums. These are delivered inside the package of a product, or they are attached to the package. Because they come with the product, in-pack and on-pack premiums provide an immediate value to the consumer and can therefore influence brand choice. They can function as tie-breakers among competing brands. The in-pack or on-pack premium can generate an impulse purchase of a brand simply because the brand selected is the only brand on the shelf offering the purchaser an added value. Useful or unique in-pack or on-pack premiums can encourage consumer trial of a brand in many product categories since the perceived value of the premium lessens the risk associated with trial.

Near-Pack Premiums. These premiums offer the consumer an immediate value, too. In this case, the promoted brand and the premium stand next to one another either on the shelf or, more commonly, in a special off-shelf display. The display can be a prepacked display shipper, or pallet, and will stay up as long as the trade is willing to allocate additional shelf or floor space to the brand. Because customer compliance with purchase requirements is hard to police and separate, display of free premiums makes them subject to theft. Retail acceptance of near-pack premiums is less than that for other kinds of premium offers. Computer coding of a foreign stock keeping unit (SKU) is frequently cited as the reason for trade reluctance to accept near-packs.

Free-in-the-Mail Premiums. This kind of premium is sent to the consumer in return for proofs of purchase. When the premium item is unusual or one that the consumer normally would not purchase, it can be an appealing reward for buying more of a routinely purchased product. Free-in-the-mail premiums encourage repeat purchase of a product by requiring multiple proofs-of-purchase. They are more effective in rewarding current users of a product than in attracting new users.

FIGURE 15–1

Nestlè Morsels Premium

Courtesy of The Nestlè Company, Inc.

Self-Liquidating Premiums. A self-liquidator is usually offered to the consumer via advertising or at the point-of-sale via the display or the product package. The consumer is required to purchase the product. With proofs-of-purchase and a cash charge, the consumer can send away for the premium and receive it in the mail (see Figure 15–1). The charge to the consumer covers the cost of the premium to the brand making the offer. At the same time, the charge to the consumer is still less than what the consumer would pay at retail and therefore represents a genuine value.

Self-liquidating premiums *do not* represent an immediate value to the consumer and do not provide a strong motivation for consumers to purchase a product. They do sustain interest in a brand when advertised, and they serve as a reward to current users of the brand. They are an inexpensive means of reinforcing a brand's advertised image when the qualities inherent in the premium reflect the attributes and imagery associated with the brand.

There are several important criteria for selecting a premium for any kind of promotion:

1. **Basic Appeal** Will customers like the premium? Will they use it, wear it, save it, or display it? Does the premium appeal more to women, to men, or to both? Will consumers say, "This gift is worth the purchase I made to get it?"
2. **Quality/Durability** The premium is an extension of the company and its products. It had better not fall apart. The color better not come out during the first washing. Aside from protecting corporate image, quality premiums telegraph a message to consumers, and that message is: "This gift is worth the purchase I made to get it."
3. **High Perceived Value** Some products and their brand names can be recognized by consumers. And consumers will know that they usually pay for those products at retail. Or they at least *sense* that the premium, by its look and feel, costs a lot. When consumers perceive a high value attached to the premium, one message comes through loud and clear: "This gift is worth the purchase I made to get it."

In the packaged goods business, a premium by itself does not dazzle the trade. But an integrated premium promotion can dazzle when it includes sell-in materials, samples for chain headquarters, loaders at the store level, point-of-purchase display materials, and plenty of advertising support.

CHAPTER 16

Sweepstakes, Games, and Contests

Everyone loves a free ride, especially in a brand new luxury automobile. And getting something free—winning extraordinarily valuable prizes—is what sweepstakes, games, and contests are all about...at least, from the consumer's point of view. As a promotional tactic, all three have climbed to unprecedented popularity over the last decade, comprising a majority of all promotions currently executed; in expenditures, all three reached an all-time high in 1984.

While winning prizes is indeed an important common denominator, laws, promotional objectives and strategies, and logistics of execution for these promotional tools vary widely. One of the central issues, of course, is the law guiding such promotions. Though rules governing sweepstakes, games, and contests differ from state to state, federal regulations apply equally everywhere: lotteries are illegal in all states. Promotion mechanics must comply with the law.

By definition, a lottery includes the elements of chance,

prizes, and consideration (i.e., a purchase). If you eliminate consideration, you have a workable and legal sweepstakes or game. If you eliminate chance, you then have a contest.

SWEEPSTAKES

The strength of sweepstakes lies in building consumer awareness of a product or service. Research shows that sweepstakes increase advertising readership; so if the goal is to heighten product/service visibility or to educate consumers about specific product/service benefits, a sweepstakes is an appropriate tactic.

Though a sweepstakes may be targeted to the consumer, it is often implemented with a view toward the trade. "Qualified," "Programmed Learning," and "Match the Display/Label" sweepstakes (see below) in particular can be used to entice the retailer to put up off-shelf displays. And since off-shelf displays can increase sales of the product displayed by as much as 1,500 percent, the sweepstakes, though it cannot require purchase, can still become a promotion of true, though indirect, pulling power.

The sweepstakes, properly executed and supported, has other attributes as well. It gives broker representatives something to talk about, facilitating their sell-in job to the retail buyer; and the evidence of strong and highly visible promotional support for a given brand has been shown to encourage retailers to stock up on the product.

The "Straight" Sweepstakes. A straight sweepstakes' objective is *solely* to heighten brand visibility and consumer awareness. All that consumers are typically required to do is complete the entry form with name and address and mail it along with one proof-of-purchase. Since purchase cannot be required, consumers may hand print the name of the product on a 3 " × 5 " card and enclose that card in lieu of the actual proof. Research shows that more than 90 percent of all entries in a straight sweepstakes are accompanied by these 3 " × 5 " "facsimiles."

There is a widely accepted belief that facsimiles lower or even eliminate people's chances of winning any major prize because an advertiser would be reluctant to hand over, say, a half-million dollars to a consumer who hasn't bought the advertiser's product. This fear has no basis in fact. To comply with the law, advertisers must treat all entries equally.

The "Qualified" Sweepstakes. This calls for consumer involvement by asking one or more questions which consumers must answer correctly in order to enter the sweepstakes drawing. Here are some popular techniques:

Programmed Learning A device encouraging consumers to read (not just scan) the body copy of the sweepstakes advertisement—which should highlight important product benefits—in order to validate the entry form with the correct answer(s). In addition to increasing brand visibility and consumer awareness, this type of sweepstakes may actually encourage nonusers to try the product by "forcing" them to learn something about a product or service they might otherwise have never discovered.

Other Entry Form Validation Techniques It is legal in most states to ask consumers to validate their entry form with an element found on the in-store display or to ask consumers to pick up the product to copy a UPC number. But our personal experience indicates that cooperating dealers are few and far between.

Match-the-Label/Display An extension of the qualified sweepstakes that crosses over into games. A match-and-win sweepstakes involves pre-seeded matching devices, such as a logo on the entry form, which have to be taken to the store and matched to the display or product. In the sweepstakes version, though, most entry forms will match, making the holder eligible for the sweepstakes drawing. Benefits of this technique are that it directs consumers to the display and/or product in the store and that it encourages off-shelf displays and sufficient inventory by the retailer. Dealer cooperation remains an issue. Such promotions are best executed with products such as beer and soft drinks where distributors can set up the necessary displays.

Automatic-Entry Coupons Of all ways to encourage coupon redemption, this is the hands-down winner. It combines a cents-off coupon with an entry form, making entering quick and easy. The consumer only needs to complete the cents-off coupon with name and address, buy the product, and redeem the coupon in doing so...a chance to win *and* a discount combined cleanly into one execution. Consumers may also enter by mailing the completed coupon, possibly with the 3 " × 5 " facsimile; but that involves getting and addressing an envelope, finding a stamp, and making a trip to the mailbox. In other words, a hassle. Even this technique, however, does not change the fact that sweepstakes are not great sales builders.

With the glut of sweepstakes currently being executed, it is a tough job to get noticed, and that's where creative positioning, theme, and prize structure must work together to maximum impact. In fact, both theme and prize structure can be worked so that they enhance, even extend, the product/service, its benefits, or a current advertising campaign for the product/service, thus making every promotion dollar work that much harder. The now-famous Benson & Hedges Deluxe 100s Sweepstakes (with total prize values far below the average) is a creative case in point and has been for 14 years. The technique used is a variation on the straight sweepstakes and provides both fun and involvement for the consumer: 100 separate sweepstakes with one prize each to choose from. The number 100 is used to highlight the brand's 100 mm length, and that idea recurs in each prize description. One-hundred mink coats, 100 pieces of sushi in Tokyo, 100 ounces of pâté de foie gras, or a computer with 100 programs are a few of the offerings.

The 1984 edition of this sweepstake classic drew a record 5 million entries and, according to Tom Keim, Director of Marketing Communications at Philip Morris, prizes and administration of the promotion cost the company less than $500,000.

GAMES

The line between sweepstakes and games is fuzzy at best, especially in the match-and-win category. As a general rule, sweepstakes determine winners by way of a drawing; games

FIGURE 16-1

7UP "Count Up Cash Not Caffeine" Game

Courtesy of The Seven-Up Company

are executed via game pieces that have to be rubbed off, matched, or collected. Game pieces are always pre-seeded— hence, the all-pervasive consumer copy approach of "You may have already won. . . ."

Because of the element of chance, as with sweepstakes, purchase cannot be required. Games, however, lend themselves to continuity. Repeat store visits and even repeat purchases are encouraged by such promotions as soft drink under-the-cap or crown games (see Figure 16-1). Mail-in alternatives to obtain game pieces make the repeat purchase inducement legal, though it is obviously easier to pick up a six-pack of Coke for six chances to win than to mail out six individual postcards for the same purpose.

The following are two popular game techniques:

Match & Win   Consumers are instructed to match a game piece (delivered via FSI or some other print medium) to store displays or to the product itself in order to learn instantly if they have won. Legally, an advertiser can require that a winning game piece be accompanied by a proof-of-purchase in order for consumers to collect their prizes. If a company has a broad prize base—i.e., many lower-level prizes—this may actually increase sales somewhat and induce trial by nonusers.

Rub & Win This has a great continuity potential and has been used widely in the fast food restaurant industry where consumers receive a game piece automatically with their visit. Game pieces are free for the asking to *everyone* who visits the store, as well. Typically, these rub & win games feature two ways to win: (1) instantly, usually low-level food prizes with any purchase during their next visit and (2) by collecting pieces to win. Consumers collect letters of a word or words comprising a phrase to win what is usually a valuable high-level prize.

The example in Figure 16–2 combines rub-off with an innovative "reveal & win" twist. For this promotion, Timex inserted pre-seeded game pieces in major consumer publications. Rub-off spots disclosed whether the card was an instant winner of one of the prizes listed in the accompanying advertisement. A "Bonus Spot" heightened the consumer's anticipation by doubling the instant winner prize if it revealed a watch face with hands exactly at 6 o'clock.

To learn whether his game piece was indeed an instant winner, the consumer had to go to a participating Timex dealer to unscramble the hidden message on the game-piece corner. To do so, he actually had to pick up a Timex watch package and look at the game piece through the colored plastic case, which screened out color obstructions and revealed the message. This is a good example of a game that gets consumers involved with the product.

Because of the excitement that they generate in the marketplace by challenging consumers to scratch, match, and collect, and because of their potential for continuity and their ability to encourage off-shelf displays, games are a

FIGURE 16–2

Timex "Accuracy Counts" Game

Courtesy of Timex Corporation

valuable promotion tool. A good deal of a game's value, of course, hinges on positioning and creative execution that mesh with the brand's or service's image, its product benefits, and its advertising.

On the other hand, games, unlike sweepstakes, require additional implementation efforts such as seeding winning game pieces and setting up security.

CONTESTS

Contests are the least utilized technique of the three consumer-participating tactics and for simple reasons: fewer consumers enter contests than games or sweepstakes, and execution of contests is time-consuming and costly. Unlike games and sweepstakes, a contest replaces chance with a skill requirement. Relatively few consumers, unfortunately, are willing to spend the time and effort necessary to enter many contests, most of which require more involvement than sweepstakes and games.

A contest thus narrows the target audience to that segment of the population with sufficient time and interest to display their "skills." Also, since chance is ruled out as a means of awarding prizes, contests require that every single entry be judged by an "independent expert," which is as time-consuming and costly as it sounds.

Some advertisers have nevertheless experienced great success with contests. Contests work well in increasing brand visibility, emphasizing product benefits, solidifying user loyalty, and getting a lot of press coverage, which translates into free advertising.

A highly successful contest, executed in 1979, was the Soft & Dri® Roll-On and Spray Deodorant "Nervous is Why . . ." contest. Print ads for this contest asked consumers to dream up a "situation" that they felt was appropriate for a Soft & Dri® TV commercial. To make things a little easier, the entry form provided examples, such as "Nervous is wearing a new string bikini . . . and the string breaks" and "Nervous is taking your driver's test . . . for the fourth time."

Consumers also had to answer three true-or-false brand benefit questions (which insured that the ad was read from top to bottom) and include either proof-of-purchase or the UPC number (which meant that even nonpurchasers had to pick up the product in-store) with their entry form.

The grand prize was to "live like a star for a week"®—a role in a Soft & Dri® TV commercial, a trip to Hollywood, a chauffeured limo, $3,000 cash, and other treats. Entries received exceeded the target objective by 236 percent, apparently because the contest possessed a combination of good characteristics: it was designed to focus on the brand's benefit, image, and advertising campaign; it struck the right chord with the target market (women); it got the advertisement read; and it encouraged purchasers and nonpurchasers to handle the product physically.

So it is possible for a contest to meet many important objectives and to make quite a splash in the marketplace; but it is also a very involved marketing tool and calls for more time-consuming administration than most forms of promotion.

It is true that sweepstakes, games, and, to a lesser degree, contests have flooded the marketplace in the last decade; but while promotion tools seem to be cyclical, recently developed techniques have greatly improved the promotional potential of these tactics. The current glut may cause advertisers to temporarily shy away from sweepstakes, games, and contests, but they will probably be important and valuable techniques in the promotional arsenal for the foreseeable future.

CHAPTER 17

Trade Shows and Sampling

TRADE SHOWS

The trade show is a marketing tool of enormous potential. It is the marketer's opportunity to "call on" all prime prospects during one "super sales call." It can be a uniquely effective marketing tool when well planned, executed, and evaluated. Too often it is an inefficient waste of resources undertaken without the proper objectives and strategies.

Trade shows are valuable for:

1. Generating qualified leads (leads that convert to sales at a higher rate, according to research, than those from other sources).
2. Sampling and demonstrating new products.
3. Reinforcing company image.

Because of declining attendance and sharply rising costs, companies are actively pursuing ways to increase performance from trade show participation.

Expected Increases in 1984 Trade Show Exhibition Costs

Component	Projected Increase in Costs
Exhibit space rental	18.7%
Hotel accommodations	12.2
Air travel	14.5
Equipment:	
Furniture rental	9.9
AV equipment rental	10.0
Services:	
Carpenter	7.7
Electrician	7.0
Plumber	8.9
Janitor	9.0
Photographer	10.6
Guard	3.3
Florist	5.6
Projectionist	6.6
Presenters/live talent	11.7
Other:	
Exhibit design, detailing	8.0
Shop construction materials	9.2
Shop construction labor	8.2
Freight	10.0
Drayage	9.9

Source: International Exhibitors Association.

There are several key steps in the planning process that can lead marketers to more productive and efficient use of trade shows.

1. Defining Your Potential Audience. What is the projected market for the product line being exhibited? Who are your prime buyers? What is their level of sophistication? Does the size of your potential audience justify participation in the show? If so, how many of your best prospects do you expect to attend?

2. Setting Objectives. Using show data and a good customer profile, a marketing manager should be able to arrive at a finite number of prime buyers who can *realistically be contacted at the show.* How many leads will be qualified? How many sales will be closed? How many prospects will be followed up?

3. Building a Strategy. Once the potential audience is defined and screened and quantifiable objectives are set, a true exhibit strategy can be created.

Key factors in trade show strategy include:

- Identifying prime prospects by name in order to invite them to your booth via direct mail before the show.
- Involving regional salespeople who can help get targeted prospects from their regions to the show.
- Planning specific demonstrations for targeted prospects.
- Using pre- and postshow advertising.
- Planning a relevant giveaway or traffic-building activity.
- Inviting prime prospects to a function (such as dinner) with top executives.
- Devising a follow-up plan.
- Devising a record-keeping system so data will be available for evaluation.

4. Designing the Exhibit. A winning approach to exhibit strategy is the problem-solving approach. Build a message that reaches out to the best prospects by hitting their "hot button," a specific problem or issue you know is important to them. Then prove that your product is the solution.

A technical demonstration is still a time-honored method of attracting buyer interest. Exhibit design is critical, ·and marketers hold different views. One school of thought advises using a design to attract only serious buyers—one that shows them the quality and professionalism of the company. Copy should be short and inviting and have a strong customer-benefit orientation. Strong corporate and product identification is another key element. Too often, as in advertising, prospects enjoy the fun but can't remember the company's name.

5. Orchestrating the Booth. Use only experienced, knowledgeable salespeople. Devise a work plan for booth personnel (four hours per shift). Give your salespeople quotas, and be sure booth personnel record key information about all prospects. (The major objective of booth personnel is to qualify prospects.)

As in direct response, exhibitors should seek only the best prospects, their buyers. Crowds merely obstruct the true, professional selling process. The real objective is to single out and establish person-to-person contact with buyers. Some exhibitors use lead forms of various designs to help them identify the prime buyer (who also must have the authority to make the purchase decision).

Today, trade show selling is becoming a "serious art" with companies instituting elaborate training programs. Such programs focus on: teaching salespeople special trade show techniques; teaching "targeting" of specific markets; teaching follow-up techniques; measuring the show's return-on-investment; improving morale and generating sales team spirit; and improving coordination of all activities.

THINGS TO AVOID

1. Show biz—entertainment won't help meet your objectives.
2. Unquantified objectives—establish a measurable objective using real numbers.
3. Attracting crowds—attract your best prospects instead.
4. The use of show biz acts, including magicians, and caricaturists—they come between you and your buyers.
5. Giveaways—they attract "collectors," not buyers.
6. Any exhibit design that's off-target with your best prospects.
7. An "untouchable" display—buyers, especially technical people, like hands-on shopping.
8. Shapes that tend to fade into the background—use geometric rather than free-form shapes.
9. Irrelevant audience participation—if used, it should revolve around product benefits.
10. Manning the booth with inexperienced salespeople or requiring shifts longer than four hours.

11. Long copy on your exhibit.
12. Emphasizing company name and deemphasizing benefit statements.
13. Spreading copy messages around the booth—keep all key benefit statements together in one area.
14. Regarding your exhibit as "cast in stone"—review your performance pattern each day and make changes to improve performance.

TRADE SHOWS—SUMMARY

Primary users of trade shows include the automotive, premium, chemical, metal, and graphic arts industries and technical, medical, and engineering manufacturers. Trade shows serve the following purposes in the marketplace. They provide for serious "comparison shopping" within various industries; they allow buyers to get first-hand technical information, often from chief engineers or other experts; and they facilitate multiple buying decisions that span a year or more.

For marketers/exhibitors, trade shows generate qualified leads, sample and demonstrate new products, reinforce company image, and provide information about buyers and the market for other marketing endeavors.

SAMPLING

Sampling is a form of sales promotion that puts the product into the hands of the ultimate consumer for the purpose of *trial* consumption. It is the most effective means of getting the consumer to try the product. Whether the product is new, a reintroduction of an "improved" product, or an old product that has a new market or new use application, sampling can boost sales and profits quickly and efficiently.

Sampling is a very expensive form of sales promotion, however, and must therefore be very well thought out, carefully executed, and justifiable in promotion plan objectives.

Sampling should be considered as a promotional tactic when a client wants to:

Introduce a new product or stimulate trial of that product.

Stimulate trial of an old product that has been improved.

Generate a new use for an existing brand or product.

Build awareness/identification for new packaging.

Introduce a brand to a new target group or through a new retail outlet.

Build or broaden a sales base in a new or weak market.

Offset a decline in market share.

Build higher and quicker initial volume levels.

Offset competitive sampling.

Various Sampling Techniques

Door-to-Door. The most common method of sampling involves placing the sample product at the door. When there is a route person, he or she rings the bell and leaves or rings the bell and hands product to the consumer with a short message. This method has great potential for selectivity within a market. However, it is very costly and requires close supervision and training of personnel. It works well for perishable or larger items that might not be delivered as efficiently by mail. Costs per unit should include all handling and warehousing.

In-Store. In in-store sampling, the sample is handed to customers in the store. This method involves relatively low distribution cost, allows for selectivity by location, and offers opportunity for a face-to-face sales message. It requires trained personnel, however, and it may miss important potential customers who are not in the store that day. The Robinson-Patman Act requires that sampling be offered to all stores on a proportionally equal basis. This method is also used in shopping malls, on the street, at transportation terminals, or in any high-traffic area.

Selective Audience. In selective audience sampling, the sample is delivered to specific groups of potential consumers—i.e., joggers, teens, mothers, or brides. Because this method is extremely selective, there is minimum waste. And because the target is so precise, results usually show a high percentage of new trials. Duplication is low, and this method is not limited to new products. Distribution programs often deliver noncompetitive product packs to high schools, maternity wards, running marathons, etc. This method shares delivery costs cooperatively and is therefore comparatively less expensive than direct-to-consumer methods. This method has little impact on the trade so it does not encourage further merchandising support.

On-/In-Pack. In this type of sampling, a trial-sized sample is attached to noncompeting or complementary product package. Distribution costs here are low. On-pack/in-pack sampling may gain an endorsement by the carrier brand and possibly even advertising support. Good shelf exposure and display from retailers could result unless the "bonus pack" is bulky and causes space problems. Distribution, though, is limited, and shelf-timing is difficult. Since this method only reaches customers carrying the product from the store, a large group of potential consumers may be missed.

Direct Mail. With direct mail sampling, an actual sample or a coupon for a free full-sized package is delivered to the consumer's home through the mail. This offers extreme selectivity, especially with a coupon, because only interested consumers will redeem them. Direct mail is an especially good method when there is simultaneous national coverage. It also provides strong trade recognition. The mailing is only as good as the mailing list, so the list must be current and on target. Bulk theft of actual samples or coupon theft is possible, as is coupon misredemption. Store support is necessary for this method to be successful. Coupon costs depend on redemption plus distribution costs for actual samples.

Sampling through Media. In media sampling, the actual sample, direct response offer, or coupon is distributed via home-delivered medium. This method has several virtues: it is easy to target by area and medium; provides immediate coverage; it has strong consumer impact; it promotes trade tie-ins; it involves no special packaging costs. The medium may charge a premium for handling the sample. Disadvantages are as follows: coupons present a potential for misredemption; write-in offers have a low level of redemption (but sample goes only to interested customers); selectivity may mean missing many potential consumers; and the method is limited to a few types of products. Costs depend on media buy, coupon redemption, product handling, and shipping.

Salable Samples. Salable samples are nominally priced trial-sized samples or free "take one" samples available through retail outlets via P.O.P. displays. This method offers mass exposure opportunities, low-cost distribution, and opportunity for profit to the trade. Special sizes require special packaging. It is not a very selective method of sampling and can be hit-or-miss as to whether target customers will take one. Also, it is difficult to determine proper quantities. The only cost is normal product distribution, so there may be room in the budget for advertising support.

Is the Product Good for Sampling?

The following product characteristics are most conducive to a successful sampling effort:

Product should be a low-priced consumption article with high volume potential and a fast rate of stock turn.

Product should be easy to package, transport, and distribute on a mass basis.

Product should offer a unique or hard-to-describe quality that is difficult to communicate verbally or orally.

Product benefits can be appreciated by using a small portion of the product.

Product has convenient retail availability so consumer is in a position to buy some soon after completed trial of the sample.

Product is demonstrably better than currently available products in the category.

Miscellaneous Planning Factors

As a brand's market share increases, sampling could become less efficient because a larger portion of the samples would go to current users. Timing is everything. New products should be sampled after sufficient advertising of the brand name so the consumer will have a greater perceived value for the sample and will be more likely to try it. If there is a seasonal sales curve for the product, samples should be delivered before the peak period. There must be ample availability of the product in the warehouses and at retail outlets. Customers who are turned on by a sample should not be turned off by unavailable product. The sample must provide enough product to allow the consumer sufficient and fair trial; however, consumers should not get so much that their initial purchase is delayed.

Examples of Sampling

In 1983, NutraSweet® (the brand name for Asparatame) began its appearance as the new sugar substitute ingredient in many new and established brands. An interesting aspect of its introduction is that consumers cannot buy NutraSweet® by itself since it is an ingredient. The G. D. Searle Company nevertheless wanted to ensure that consumers would accept NutraSweet® and buy the products that contained it.

The product claimed to be as sweet as sugar, without the calories and without the aftertaste associated with saccharin. Introductory advertisements explained the product, described the benefits, and instructed the reader to look for products with the NutraSweet® brand name on the package. The copy closed with this statement: "Because when you find it, you'll love how NutraSweet® makes food taste."

Sampling, of course, was obviously the appropriate sales promotion choice to support and communicate this all-important advertising claim. Because NutraSweet® had to be tasted to be believed, the advertisement included a direct response form for customers to mail in for their free sample. The creative choice for delivering the taste was a very appropriate one: five gumballs sweetened with NutraSweet®. This provided a simple way to invite consumers to decide for themselves.

That sampling effort contributed substantially to the success of NutraSweet® which is now well known in the food and beverage industries.

As reported in the May 9, 1983 edition of *Advertising Age,* service companies are also taking advantage of the rewards of sampling. MCI Telecommunications offered the "Free Holiday Call" to holiday shoppers in 160 malls and department stores. The company invited people to make a free three-minute long-distance call from a booth installed at each location. By asking each caller to provide a name, address, and telephone number, local MCI sales representatives were able to follow up and convert trials into new subscribers. Local advertising and publicity supported the effort.

This promotion took place in 1982. By 1985, as Equal Access (a program that will eventually eliminate multiple-digit dialing for various long-distance services) came into effect, MCI offered more "free samples" to existing customers. To induce them to inform local telephone companies that MCI was their official choice for Dial-1 service, MCI offered 60 free minutes of long-distance calls.

The Donnelley *Marketing Newsletter,* November 1984, reported that Del Monte used in-store sampling to introduce five new fruit nectar flavors targeted directly at the fast-growing Hispanic market. The company selected Miami (Cuban) and New York (Puerto Rican) as its two test markets. After demographic analyses, Donnelley Marketing identified geographic areas with large Hispanic populations and high-volume supermarkets. The Del Monte sales force then sold the product line with commitments for product displays. The company used bilingual demonstrators in their sampling program. Results revealed the trial-to-conversion rate to be among the highest achieved in Donnelley's sampling experience.

A Final Word about Sampling

Success in sampling depends on planning and coordinating a multitude of factors. Cost efficiency is evaluated by how well the plan justifies preset objectives. Additional advertising and sales promotion support will also bear on the outcome and should be considered if budget allows. Companies must consider how the trade is affected by sampling efforts and make sure the product really needs to be sampled in order to communicate its benefits to the consumer.

Sampling is a highly effective sales promotion tool and communicates more about a product than words or pictures. However, it is the most expensive form of sales promotion and must be used wisely to produce profitable results.

CHAPTER 18

Tie-in/Group Promotions

Over the last decade, more and more companies have come to rely on tie-in or group promotions to carry a substantial portion of the sales promotion load.[1] *A tie-in pools resources of two or more brands to promote a consumer offer and/or event under a common theme.*

This trend may be attributed to two influences: (1) in recent years, there has been a resurgence of promotional tactics that are unaffordable on a single-brand basis; and (2) more demands are being placed on sales departments so they have less time to devote to single-brand promotions.

While specific objectives vary, the basic goals of a tie-in or group promotion are generally related to its promotional tactic. For example, when three brands jointly promote a sweepstakes, the basic objectives should be those that a sweepstakes event is designed to achieve. A tie-in, moreover, can incorporate any standard promotional tactic; it can be as simple as cross-ruff couponing (where one brand carries the coupon of another brand either in- or on-pack) or as complex as multimedia, multibrand executions targeted at the trade or consumer.

ADVANTAGES

Properly executed and well-presented, tie-ins can be more effective than solo promotional events. While the preliminary leg work is greater than that associated with single-brand promotions, tie-ins offer participants a multitude of benefits.

Reduced Delivery Costs. Although participants generally cover their own redemption costs, the overall expense of delivering the event is shared. Costs associated with advertising, point-of-sale materials, and promotional overlays are always negotiated prior to the event.

Higher-Value Incentives. The combined budget of two or more brands enables participants to offer higher-value consumer incentives that are generally unaffordable on a single-brand basis.

Greater Trade Support. When two or more brands join together under a common theme, the trade is more likely to support the promotion with feature ads and/or in-store merchandising.

Increased Advertising Value. In targeting the audience of each participating brand, tie-in promotions reach a greater number of potential buyers.

Greater Sales Force Support. The trade "sell-in" of a tie-in is generally more successful than that of a single-brand event because more than one sales force is promoting the effort.

New Distribution. Tie-ins can be an effective tool for gaining new distribution of partner products. Let's say, for example, that a media-supported tie-in features products A, B, and C and that the trade carries only products A and B. The tie-in event provides leverage for selling product C.

Expanded Product Usage. Joint promotion of related products can suggest new product uses. An example of this is a recipe tie-in that links various food products.

Enhanced Product Image. Endorsement is implicit when one product teams up with another. A relatively new product in the marketplace can benefit from association with well-established partner products.

DISADVANTAGES

While there are many benefits from implementing a tie-in promotion, there are three primary drawbacks to consider.

Tedious Partner Selection Process. The process of selecting tie-in partners that are both compatible and complementary can be quite time-consuming. While there are no absolute guidelines, partner products should have similar target audiences, and all participants should benefit from the venture.

Greater Preliminary Leg Work. Tie-ins require greater lead time than solo events because there is much more initial planning. When multiple brands or companies are involved, reaching an agreement regarding costs and execution is often quite time-consuming.

Less Individuality. A tie-in theme (promoting multiple products) often overpowers the sales message of individual participants.

GUIDELINES

A number of guidelines are useful in planning a successful tie-in event:

- The partner selection process should flow naturally from the nature of the event, so a theme and offer should be developed *before* grouping.
- The event should be anchored with at least one large, established brand because smaller brands need a sizable trade merchandising base to build on.

- The promotional overlay and tie-in theme should be correct strategically and tactically for each brand.

- The promotional overlay should be simple so the sales force and trade can focus their attention easily.

- If possible, each tie-in promotion should be tested before it is implemented on a national basis.

- Media support should be secured to heighten consumer interest in the event.

- Tie-in promotions should not take the place of more focused solo events because too many group promotions can detract from a brand's individuality.

- An outside source should be considered to help handle negotiations and arrangements. Outsiders can bring objectivity to the event, and they have the time that may not be available internally.

CASE HISTORIES

These three case histories exemplify successful tie-in events:

Promotion/Theme:	GET 'EM WHILE THEY'RE HOT WHEELS®!
Partners:	McDonald's® Corporation and Mattel® Toy Company
Objectives:	*McDonald's*—to increase topline sales and transactions by 9 percent and 5 percent, respectively.
	Mattel—to increase awareness and trial of Hot Wheels Cars.
Activity:	*Self-Liquidated Premium Offer*
	A different Hot Wheels car was offered each day for 59 cents plus tax with purchase (limit one car per food item purchased). The offer was communicated in approximately 5,800 McDonald's restaurants nationwide for a period of four weeks.
Implementation:	The Hot Wheels line of toy cars offered built-in continuity and collectability. Fourteen different Hot Wheels cars were offered for the first two weeks of the promotion (see Figure 18–1). Then,

FIGURE 18-1

McDonald's and Mattel Hot Wheels Promotion

Courtesy of McDonald's Corporation

	for the last two weeks, the order of rotation was changed in order to insure that the same car was never offered on the same day of the week throughout the promotion. Mattel also offered customers rebates on five different Hot Wheels Accessory Kits, and rebate forms were available in each McDonald's Restaurant.
Results:	The promotion exceeded expectations. All reporting stores sold out all of their Hot Wheels cars. Sales increased in excess of 11 percent, and transactions increased in excess of 5 percent. The average store sold over 1,500 cars per week.
Promotion/Theme:	DURACELL® HOME IMPROVEMENT REBATE PROMOTION
Partners:	Duracell and 14 home improvement product marketers

Objectives:	*Duracell*—to increase topline sales, to build brand awareness, and to generate trade merchandising support.
	Partners—to increase brand awareness, to cultivate new users, to generate repurchase, and to capitalize on the Duracell name.
Activity:	*Rebate Offer*
	Positioned as a spring home improvement campaign, the promotion featured discounts on a wide range of products used for cleaning, gardening, and home repair. Valued at over $125, the Duracell Home Improvement Rebate Certificate offered refunds on 20 different products.
Implementation:	The offer was communicated via four-color, freestanding inserts delivered in more than 150 Sunday newspapers with a combined circulation of 41 million. Each insert featured two coupons, one for 25 cents off the list price of Duracell batteries, the other an order form requiring two proofs-of-purchase to receive the Duracell Home Improvement Rebate Certificate. In assuming the total cost of producing, printing and placing the insert, Duracell offered participants a high visibility promotion at a relatively low cost. Individual participants were responsible only for their own fulfillment costs. To create additional awareness at the point of purchase, the Rebate Certificate order form was also printed on in-store, tear-off pads and shelf talkers.
Results:	Within five days after the coupons started coming in, approximately 100,000 order forms for Rebate Certificates had been received. While requests for the Rebate Certificate are still being tallied, the overall response rate is estimated at 1 percent, which is much higher than the average 0.7 percent to 0.9 percent response rate on liquidators.

| Promotion/Theme: | "WHEN THE U.S. WINS, YOU WIN" |
| Partners: | McDonald's® Corporation and the U.S. Olympic Committee |

Objectives: *McDonald's*—(1) To demonstrate leadership in the fast-service restaurant category without resorting to tactics used by its competitors, (2) to increase store sales by 5 percent and store transactions by 8 percent, (3) to encourage television viewing of the Summer Olympics, thereby increasing the impact of its heavy TV buy.

Activity: *"Free" Rub-Off Game*

During the Games, McDonald's distributed "When the U.S. Wins, You Win" game cards to every customer (no purchase was necessary). Each card had a rub-off spot that revealed the name of an Olympic event. If the United States won a gold medal in that event, the holder of the card won a Big Mac® sandwich. A silver medal won the holder an order of french fries, and a bronze medal won the holder a soft drink (see Figure 18–2).

FIGURE 18–2

McDonald's "When the U.S. Wins You Win!" Promotion

Courtesy of McDonald's Corporation

Implementation: Customers visited McDonald's Restaurants to get game cards and play along with the events as they were broadcast on television. Because Olympic medal winners were also posted daily in each store, customers would make return visits in order to find out if they held winning game cards, to get additional game cards, or to redeem any winning cards they might have.

Results: Participation levels by store owner/operators were the highest in McDonald history. During the six-week promotional period, over 300 million game cards were distributed, and total store sales and transactions increased by 5.8 percent and 11.2 percent, respectively.

CHAPTER 19

Continuity
and Stamp Programs

A continuity program is basically an attempt to "hook" a customer for a short period, thus building up shopping habits that it is hoped will continue even after the program has ended.

The customer typically must accumulate something—stamps, register tapes, points, labels, proofs-of-purchase—that may be used in a specific quantity either to purchase something at a reduced price or to receive it free.

Continuity programs are most successful when they offer a much-needed or much-coveted product or service at a great perceived value and when they are unique in the market.

In supermarket chains, which frequently use tape-saver continuity programs to gain customers and sales, this uniqueness can mean the difference between a successful program and a failure. In 1984, Jewel Food Stores, a large, Illinois-based chain, ran a save-a-tape program for telephones just as the public telephone company in that region ceased to require that residents lease their telephones exclusively. Each resident had the option of purchasing a telephone either from the telephone company or from an independent source. Jewel had given the public a timely option, a wide range of telephones at outstanding values with an appropriate number of Jewel register tapes. The program was a great success.

Small appliances, lawn furniture, luggage, wristwatches, gold jewelry, and pots and pans are other items that have been successfully offered on supermarket save-a-tape plans.

As *Incentive Marketing* reported (November 1982), even banks have successfully offered continuity programs of one sort or another. Continental Federal Savings and Loan in Cleveland, Ohio offered china and crystal glassware to encourage steady deposits from its customers. After an opening deposit got them started, customers could purchase seven items for their set with each subsequent $25 deposit.

The structure of the Continental offer differs from typical tape-saver type plans in that the reason to return again is *not* to accumulate receipts or points, but to accumulate a full set of something. Frequently, with such plans, the first item in the set is offered at a remarkable value; subsequent weeks' items cost a set price with a transaction at the store (or bank or restaurant).

This is called a collection continuity program. Typical offerings include table settings of china or stoneware, flatware, decorated glasses, fine crystal, books that come in a series (such as encyclopedias), or "chapters" of a book in looseleaf form. In the last instance, the consumer will eventually collect a whole bookful of craft ideas, home repair tips, holiday recipes, etc.

Many questions must be addressed before setting up a merchandise-based continuity program.

- Can the company maintain a long-term program? Can it maintain displays? Will the company be able to afford regular advertising for the program? Most of these plans at the retail level run 10 to 15 weeks.
- Does the target audience perceive the offered item as a

value? Do people like it? Focus group testing might be a worthwhile investment since a carelessly chosen item sometimes does more harm than good.

- Can the company adequately warehouse sufficient quantities of the item(s)? Does the company have return privileges in case of surplus at the program's end? Can it reorder more product in time if supplies run low? Does the company have adequate personnel to do all the bookwork involved in tracking inventories?
- How will fulfillment be handled? Will it be handled through stores or the mail with a redemption center?

Because of the many complications involved, some firms hire companies that are in the business of running continuity programs. They are set up precisely for this purpose and will provide packaged plans or work with firms to develop a customized program.

In the past few years, a new marketing concept has emerged in this area: service continuities. These programs are designed to keep customers returning to a given provider. Among the current examples of service continuities, two are notable:

- **Frequent Flyer Programs** offered by airlines. As customers accumulate mileage on a particular carrier, they can earn merchandise rewards (such as cameras, electronics, and video equipment) or, more common, free trips on that carrier.
- **Frequent Visitor Programs** offered by hotels. Rewards may include free or discounted stays of varying durations, flight discounts on a certain airline, and rental car deals. The possibilities for tie-ins are innumerable and depend only on the willingness of the tie-in partners and the creativity of the provider.

In both of these examples, the more loyal (frequent) a customer, the better his rewards. Thus, with each stay or each flight, the customer is not only getting a chance for a better reward, the company is also reducing the likelihood of the customer switching to another provider since that would inhibit the cumulative effects of his continuity of use.

There are, finally, on-pack and in-pack continuity type programs. The former generally consists of labels to collect and mail in for a premium advertised on the package; the latter generally consists of a premium (part of a series) that is tucked into the package. These types of continuities have been used successfully for years with frequently purchased items and brands. Betty Crocker's program of labels for stainless flatware and Campbell Soup's program of labels for school equipment were both long-running successes.

STAMP PROGRAMS

Trading stamps rise and fall in usage but have been around since the 1890s when the Edward Schuster Company (now Gimbel's) began to use them. The most common form of trading stamps are those issued and redeemed by one company but distributed by many companies. This is the way Sperry & Hutchinson (S&H) green stamps work. Collectors are given stamp books and are able to trade filled stamp books for merchandise from a catalog issued by the stamp company. The more books that a person has filled, the more valuable the merchandise he is eligible for. At the height of the trading stamp era, the 1960s, there were between 350 and 400 stamp companies doing business, according to Stanley Ulanoff's *Handbook of Sales Promotion.* In 1981, there were fewer than 100 such companies, and 70 percent of all stamp business was done by the top five companies.

Stamps are seen by store customers as a value-added reason to patronize a place of business. According to Ulanoff, customers most likely to save stamps have traditionally been those with the least amounts of discretionary income. And, as Schultz and Robinson observe in *Sales Promotion Essentials,* trading stamp programs are usually long term and, for that reason, not very practical in packaged goods sales promotions.

It is possible, however, to construct a viable promotion by issuing product-specific stamps that are received with a purchase and collected on a card until the card is filled. The card then may be redeemed for a merchandise award. A retailer could fulfill the reward right at the store, or a product manufacturer could handle redemption through the mail. A program like this works essentially the same as a tape-saving or label-saving plan. Here again, the services of a company dealing in continuity programs may be employed to run the program and/or its fulfillment.

CHAPTER 20

Bonus Packs/Price-Offs

Every good marketing textbook tells us that four principal elements make up the marketing mix. They are referred to as the four Ps—product, place, price, and promotion. Over the years, we have seen that price has become the most important ingredient in the promotion mix.

THE BONUS PACK

In the Middle Ages, the baker who offered the 13th bun was probably the father of the bonus pack. The bonus pack is a form of price promotion. It offers additional product at or below the regular unit price. By showing a direct price-value relationship at the point-of-purchase, the marketer can make the bonus pack an effective promotion technique.

There are a number of ways to implement the bonus pack, but the most common form in the packaged goods business is extra ounces, pounds, or product. Recently, Heinz Tomato

Ketchup offered extra ounces in its family-size pack; One-A-Day Brand vitamins offered 40 extra vitamin pills free with the purchase of a regular quantity of 100 vitamins.

Bonus packs are also commonly used for tobacco or soap products—extra packages of cigarettes are banded onto cartons or several bars of soap are banded together for the price of two. Some of these techniques are powerful, particularly when they are used with a product that has strong consumer appeal, good advertising, and an established price-value relationship.

Too frequently clients request bonus pack promotions on little-known or poorly-distributed products and are disappointed when the promotion fails. Unless the products are well-entrenched in the marketplace, and unless the price-value relationship is clearly established in the minds of the consumer, the success rate of bonus packs is frequently less than the marketer anticipates. Also, retailers are less motivated to promote products whose demand is not clearly identified.

If the brand is well-known and well-advertised, however, the retailer is quick to provide the kind of support that ensures the program's success. The retailer may feature the product or the bonus pack in his advertising and will frequently provide off-shelf displays and price features within the store. The bottom line is that, if the retailer is convinced the consumer can recognize the value, he will support the product and/or the promotion. On the other hand, if the retailer thinks that the brand is not well-known or that the price-value is not clearly established, he will be less likely to support it. In reality, most major brands offer some kind of bonus pack or price-off promotion. (The on-pack and in-pack premiums, other forms of the bonus pack, are discussed in the chapter on premiums.)

INTERNAL PROBLEMS—BONUS PACKS

One problem that should be considered (although it is less frequently encountered today than it was in the past) involves the inventory control and warehousing systems of many packaged goods companies. Most bonus packs and/or prepack displays require special SKUs, the inventory numbering system used by the retailer. And additional computer entries and special identification numbers can cause some confusion in warehouses.

Today, most sophisticated marketers in the packaged goods business have solved the computer problem and are willing and conditioned to accept bonus packs and prepacks without a major disruption in their bookkeeping and inventory control systems.

A manufacturer can incur some hidden costs when putting together a bonus pack. Sometimes management neglects to consider the cost of altering production and packaging when budgeting for a bonus pack promotion. This is good news for marketers in companies that view any alteration in package, package design, outer carton, or shipping carton as a manufacturing or packaging expense and not as a promotion expense. However, such a disruption in the manufacturing process is really a promotion expense and should be looked on as such.

Time may be another cost element in the process of creating bonus packs. If packaging must be redesigned and reordered, enough time must be allowed not only to accommodate that need but also to change the production and packing lines to accommodate the change in procedure. Regardless of how powerful the promotion idea may be, if the manufacturing process is too disrupted, the cost of the promotion will be thrown off.

Similar time problems can occur with noted price promotions (i.e., price promotions that are on-pack) and with bonus packs when appropriate trade support materials are needed. Newspaper advertisements, radio scripts, and point-of-sale materials all need time to be completed so that the bonus pack (or price pack) can be featured.

THE PRICE-OFF OR PRICE PACK

Price-offs and price packs are another major tool used by both manufacturers and retailers today. Price-offs are offered on a continuing basis to the retail trade; yet only a small percentage of those special product prices are passed on to the consumer. On the other hand, almost any time a product is featured at retail, it is supported by a special manufacturer's pricing promotion.

Some manufacturers alter their packaging in order to ensure that price discounts are passed on to the consumer. Most commonly a color burst on the package will announce 25 cents or 10 cents off the regular price. Some retailers take serious exception to this kind of promotion, while others readily accept it. Retailers like to keep control of the kind of pricing they pass through to the consumer. On the other hand, a discount of 10 cents or more on a prelabeled product is usually more than offset by the depth of the discount at wholesale. Usually, if the discount is 10 cents per pack, the wholesale discount is proportionately greater and therefore encourages the retailer to pass on the savings. In some instances, the entire amount of the price reduction is covered by the cost of the lower deal to the trade.

"REGULAR" PRICE

In advertising sections of local newspapers, two food products are commonly featured by the leading stores—soft drinks and frankfurters. The price-off is probably the most frequently used promotion in the soft drink business, though it is usually difficult to identify the real price for soft drinks. In many cases, the "regular" price is a mystery, and real prices are usually disclosed only for lesser-known brands and less frequently purchased sizes.

FACTORY-AUTHORIZED PRICE-OFFS

Factory-authorized sales are another form of price-off promotion used in the hard goods industry—specifically for appliances and automobiles. That industry has had a long history of aggressively supporting manufacturers' promotions at retail including factory-authorized price promotions or special event promotions, such as those for President's Day, Fourth of July, Memorial Day, or Labor Day.

SHORT LIFE CYCLE VERSUS LONG
LIFE CYCLE

Certain products have short life cycles. Each life cycle is a direct function of the availability of the product in the home. Snack foods and soft drinks are good examples of products with short life cycles. So price promotions usually result in short-term incremental business. Yet, there are other products with long consumption cycles, and companies should not be deluded by short-term success in those instances. The longer-term purchase—i.e., repeat purchase of more slowly consumed products—is a more accurate indicator of success. All products have their own consumption patterns, of course, and experience with specific products will naturally influence how success is measured.

THE CAVEATS

As with any tactic, bonus packs and price-offs can be over used. Excessive use of either tactic may delude consumers' perceptions and attitudes toward a brand. Judicious use, on the other hand, may enhance the consumers' perceptions of a brand. In 1984, Frankel & Company's Stopping Power of Promotion survey (mentioned previously with other tactics) tested both bonus packs and price packs. Results showed that consumer perception of a brand improved with these promotions contrasted with advertising not supported by bonus packs and price-offs.

The major danger of straight price promotion is that competitors can respond quickly. If a secondary brand is starting to cut into the position of a primary brand, the price promotion will either be matched or beaten by the stronger competitor. The current battle between Coca Cola and Pepsi Cola for retailer attention is price-centered and has had a major impact on the profitability of bottlers of other soft drinks. Similarly, when Maxwell House and Folger's began their price warfare, secondary brands in the coffee business were frequently hurt the most.

While price promotion is effective, it is also the kind of promotion that can be easily matched by the competition. Managers should have a pretty good feel for, and be reasonably sensitive to, the reaction that a promotion of this nature will generate in the marketplace.

CHAPTER 21

Point-of-Purchase

The point of sale is where everything comes together. The product that research worked years to develop; the package that was created to communicate the product's positioning and to make it accessible for the consumer to use; the distribution system that was designed to ensure product availability in the appropriate classes of trade; the pricing strategy, the advertising, the promotion, and the trade deal that were designed to convey the product's high quality and reasonable price; the warehousing systems that had to be accommodated; the sales force that had to be trained to persuade the trade to accept the product all culminate in the final presentation of the product to the consumer. All this and more is done so that at the right time, in the right size, in the right color, at the right price, and at the right place, the product is at the point of sale.

This is the point of fruition for the manufacturer. It is the ultimate test. Will sales increase from the in-store display?

Primary Reasons for Unplanned Purchases

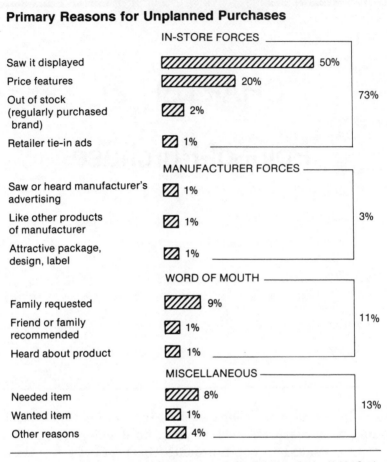

IN-STORE FORCES

Saw it displayed	50%
Price features	20%
Out of stock (regularly purchased brand)	2%
Retailer tie-in ads	1%

73%

MANUFACTURER FORCES

Saw or heard manufacturer's advertising	1%
Like other products of manufacturer	1%
Attractive package, design, label	1%

3%

WORD OF MOUTH

Family requested	9%
Friend or family recommended	1%
Heard about product	1%

11%

MISCELLANEOUS

Needed item	8%
Wanted item	1%
Other reasons	4%

13%

Source: The Point-Of-Sale Advertising Institute, *DuPont Consumer Buying Habits Study.*

Evidence supports the concept that the point of sale may be the most important component of the entire marketing chain. The Point-of-Sale Advertising Institute reported in its *Du-Pont Consumer Buying Habits Study* that 64.8 percent of supermarket purchase decisions are made at the point of sale—almost two thirds of all such decisions. This includes substitutes and planned buys in which the shopper has an item in mind, but no brand. This is the environment in which manufacturers must make in-store display decisions. In-store display increases product movement.

To assess display impact, *Progressive Grocer* conducted the

Dillon Study (January 1960), which attempted to measure increase in sales due to in-store display for the week the displays were set up. An analysis of sales of 360 items on 734 display exposures in five supermarkets brought the following results: "Unit sales of the average item featured at a reduced price jumped 808 percent. Dollar sales increased 442 percent. Unit sales of the average item featured on special display at its regular shelf price jumped 473 percent. Dollar sales increased 426 percent."

The A&P study conducted by *Progressive Grocer* in 1972 also indicated the impact on sales for a small number of items not specified by brand. The study showed that advertising and display together create "629 percent more sales than normal" and that display alone (without advertising) creates a 420 percent increase in normal movement. This information seems consistent with the Dillon study findings; it is tangible evidence that special display can and does significantly affect unit sales. Frankel & Company's more recent experience indicates sales increases up to 2,300 percent as a result of special display with no advertising.

Other experience indicates that consumers expect special displays to offer price-reduced products, and they don't take the time really to compare prices. A tradition of low prices for displayed products leads people to believe that products on display are generally price-reduced.

From all appearances, the rush is on to get display feature in supermarkets. However, there are approximately 10,000 different products in the average supermarket, and, depending on the retailer, as few as 10 can be featured at one time. In addition, many retailers have established policies against using manufacturer-provided point-of-purchase materials. So the most imaginatively created materials may be of no influence in many outlets. On the other hand, all other marketing components being equal, well-designed and executed P.O.P. materials can be an important influence in the selection of one brand over another for special display feature (see Figure 21–1). Well-designed display material is only one ingredient involved in encouraging retail support. *The use of manufacturer-created materials is not the issue; the special display feature is.*

FIGURE 21–1

Examples of Point-of-Purchase Displays

Courtesy of The Parker Pen Company   Courtesy of Citibank N.A.

SOME CRITERIA RETAILERS USE TO SELECT FEATURE PRODUCT

With over 10,000 products to choose from, with most products today at parity with others in their category, with the proliferation of deal, the real selling muscle has transferred from the brand to the retailer. In addition, the retailer has to compete with other retailers and select feature product that will enhance his position in the market. Profit is not the only criterion.

Charles H. Jenkins, Sr., Publix's Chairman of the Board,

FIGURE 21–1 *(concluded)*

Courtesy of Hueblein Inc.

believes "to be really effective, merchandising must do more than promote. It should also keep customers informed, assist in their buying decisions, and help make shopping more convenient, exciting, and pleasant."

Retailers use the following considerations to select feature products.

1. Is this the brand that my shoppers ask for regularly? It is more effective to promote the products my customers purchase regularly.
2. Is this brand perceived as being as good as or better than other brands in the category?
3. Is there a logical reason for promoting this brand or category? There should be a rational seeking theme that emanates naturally from the promotion idea, preferably one that is expandable to other products or categories.
4. Is the deal appealing? Seldom, if ever, will retailers support or promote product offered at regular price. Some consumer discounts are less than those offered the trade; conversely, retailers use promotions to build store traffic

and will offer consumer discounts that exceed their own deals.

5. Is the national advertising or promotion strong enough to influence my customers? Can I use either as a selling reason?

6. Will local support plans, materials, and co-op funds support me as well as the brand? Remember that the retailers are as competitive in their markets as the manufacturers are in their categories.

7. Will point-of-sale materials reflect my image as well as the brand's? Will they be informative to the consumer? Are the materials simple to assemble and usable in a retail environment?

8. What is the profit potential for providing in-store display support?

9. Will the promotion of the offered brand enhance the shopping experience of my customers?

The decision to support a given brand must go through an extensive screen. There is no magical formula to ensure retail support.

RANDOM DISPLAY SITUATIONS

Store-delivered products (e.g., soft drinks and snack foods) are treated somewhat differently at the point of sale. Because these products are "detailed" by the vendor, they frequently have added flexibility in the use of point-of-sale materials. Special in-store features are sometimes arranged a year in advance, and companies know when brands are to be featured. Such deals are frequently based on predetermined schedules of wholesalers, and, in return, the retailer guarantees to feature the product at an established promotional price.

Cigarette and some cosmetic companies purchase display space from the retailer, who guarantees numbers of facings and consistent locations. Cigarette carton racks are usually owned by one manufacturer, who gives them to the retailer, who in turn charges each brand a monthly fee for facings. The company that supplies the rack enjoys first-choice position.

In addition to their value as promotion feature mechanisms, point-of-sale materials all need to dispense, distribute, display, demonstrate, sample, organize, and simplify selection or information.

Point-of-sale material is frequently an essential component of the selling package. Greeting cards are sold from manufacturer-supplied fixtures. Some fixtures are given free of charge to the retailer; others are sold to the trade through a variety of innovative deals and financing plans. A similar merchandising system is used for the distribution and sale of hand tools. Battery racks are usually manufacturer-supplied to hang a comprehensive inventory of batteries in supermarkets, drug chains, and mass merchandisers.

In some high-tech industries, point-of-sale material is used to demonstrate product. For example, the interactive, touch-screen video is commonly used in auto dealerships and banks. Stereo speaker and component demonstration centers are commonly used to help consumers select components best suited to their needs. Most of the better retail component sales organizations have such systems available.

Most paint stores have color selection systems where special sections of prepainted samples are available to help purchasers organize color schemes. Carpeting sample racks have become standard for displaying, selling, and selecting carpeting. Many of these displays, fixtures, signs, etc., are as important as sales tools as they are as aids to color or style selection. Properly organized, all the salient benefits of the product can be included to assist retail salespeople in their presentations of the product's features. Mannington Mills Compu-Flor, for example, a small computerized display placed in floor covering retail outlets, is programmed to use a potential consumer's answers to eight questions about room decor. The terminal then displays 3 to 10 appropriate Mannington styles for the customer to choose from. When idle, the machine beeps periodically to attract consumers. By the end of 1982, Mannington had placed the units in 700 stores at a cost of $8 million—an amount equal to the company's advertising budget.

Mannington found that Compu-Flor selected styles for customers more efficiently than salespeople (who had trouble remembering all the styles in the product line), encouraged salespeople to push Mannington products rather than those of its two larger competitors, Armstrong and Congoleum, and boosted the number of sales closed on a customer's first store visit.

Compu-Flor is just one of a number of computerized video displays at the point of purchase that provides a standard controllable message from manufacturer to consumer and a way of engaging customers' attention while they are waiting for sales assistance.

The world's most sophisticated vending machine, the ATM (Automatic Teller Machine), now makes it possible for us to do our banking without visiting the bank. From remote locations, we can make deposits, get cash, and transfer money from one account to another.

APPENDIX

Probably the best way to understand the immense task involved in implementing a promotional tactic is to view it from the perspective of this Audience-Action Chart. The chart shows the two basic contentions that we have emphasized in this book: (1) the labor-intensive quality of all non-media marketing and (2) the extent of human media involved in a seemingly uncomplicated tactic fulfillment.

But is it uncomplicated? All that is being asked of consumers is that they take advantage of a coupon offer, that they make a purchase, consume the product, and make ultimate use of the coupon. Consumers' awareness is limited to the coupon's appearance either in a newspaper or a national advertisement, to the product appearing in an off-shelf display erected and filled by an aisle clerk.

From the perspective of the manufacturer's marketing management, the process is far more complicated. The chart simplifies a most perplexing arrangement of details.

Though management's discussion and direct relationship is with its own sales force, it must nevertheless make *all the media plans and create all the tactics* to motivate to a predictable action all those individuals at each step along the way—the management sales force, the wholesaler, the retailer, and all others connected to them—who will influence the sale of the product through the use of that coupon.

The chart should be viewed from the bottom up. A logical start would be in the Media column. The chart details those

Audience	Desired Action	Tactic	Media	Responsibility Fulfillment
Consumer	Purchase Consume	Coupon	Display Newspaper National advertising	Aisle clerk Trade management Redemption center
Retailer	Advertising Display Feature	Deal (T.A.) Promo funding	Trade publicity Wholesaler sales Buying committee presentation	Wholesaler sales Wholesaler principle
Wholesaler	Support program Present program Fund program	Volume discount New distributor incentive	National meeting Filmed presentation	Corporate sales Corporate marketing
Sales force	Inform and ARM wholesalers Feedback Develop wholesaler/ retailer plans	Commission and special incentives Annual bonus	Sales meeting Presentation of all selling and promotion tools	Sales management Marketing management (promo)
Management	Finance and support program	Pro forma of accomplishment Management recognition	Management presentation	Corporate management

media selected by management to do the intended job at each level in the distribution chain. In the Tactic column are those tactics used to motivate people at each corresponding level to perform the tasks indicated in the Desired Action column. Listed in the right-hand column are those individuals or departments whose responsibility is fulfillment.

Do all tactics require the same amount of work? Could a chart of this kind be created for all tactics? All tactics do, indeed, require the same amount of work in one form or another. A similar chart *could* be created for each tactic; but depending on such variables as the kind of product, media tie-in, distribution pattern, and trade relationships, emphasis would probably vary.

Part IV

Considerations

CHAPTER 22

Long-Term versus Short-Term Planning

Although marketers who invent a product or product category start out with no competition, they may soon find themselves facing a fierce competitive environment.

At one time Michelin manufactured the only radial tire, and in 1970 Michelin's total advertising budget was approximately $280,000. In 1979, Michelin spent $6,200,000 to compete with companies such as Firestone, Goodrich, Goodyear, Montgomery Ward, Sears, and Uniroyal.

In 1955, McDonald's was the first fast-food franchise with nationwide locations. In 1970, it spent $18 million on advertising. But to compete with at least 30 competitors, such as Burger King, Wendy's, and Arby's, McDonald's spent $140 million on advertising in 1979.

In 1964, General Foods introduced Maxim—the first freeze-dried coffee. Until recently, Polaroid was the only company manufacturing an instant camera. For both General Foods and Polaroid, competitive situations have changed significantly, and so have advertising budgets needed to increase product awareness.

Today's companies must find new ways to attract consumers. Promotion growth indicates that companies are indeed using more techniques. Couponing, for example, once restricted to the grocery business, has found its way into many business categories. According to A. C. Nielsen, the number of companies using coupons has grown from 350 in 1962 to over 1,000 today.

How a marketer allocates dollars to promotion and advertising is becoming increasingly important. One frequently occurring problem is that companies do not integrate promotion with other marketing goals. The advertising program is planned on an annual long-term basis, and promotion is added as an afterthought.

Furthermore, in most companies, advertising budgets are the result of painstaking research, planning, and development. Promotion budgets, by contrast, are seldom given the same attention. In fact, promotion expenditures often pass unnoticed because of wide variations in accounting practices—free goods are sometimes viewed as discounts, extra ounces are considered a manufacturing expense, and the cost of special packs or labels is buried in packaging expenses. There must be a better way for marketers to get more effective return on their promotion investment.

To illustrate a better way of developing a promotion plan, let's compare the planning sequence used for advertising to the one typically used for a promotion plan. Although this comparison is necessarily a simplification, a model for promotional planning should be standard procedure regardless of product, company size, or competitive conditions.

Advertising	**Promotion**

1. Background review
    a. Target
    b. Position
    c. History
    d. Competition
    e. Research
    f. Other
	1. Review the historical promotion time periods and determine the budget.

Advertising	Promotion
2. Set primary creative objective as it relates to overriding marketing objectives and strategy.	2. Establish a general objective (be competitive) and strategy (and offer competitive allowances).
3. Set creative strategy.	3. Schedule promotions by region and time period.
4. Review with top management and make necessary modifications.	4. Submit as a small part of total marketing plan.
5. Establish the advertising theme, unique selling propositions, tone, etc.	5. Create promotion themes based on time periods as you go through year.
6. Review with management and make necessary changes.	6. Maybe review with top management. If done, the basis of discussion is usually limited to financial planning.
7. Set the creative budget and develop executions for the entire year. This step includes writing copy, establishing graphics, copy testing, developing the actual ads and commercials, etc.	7. No comparable promotion step.
8. Establish media objectives including reach, frequency, and Gross Rating Points, to be specified over the entire year.	8. No comparable promotion step.
9. Establish media strategy, which includes defining specific mediums, scheduling audience, etc.	9. No comparable promotion step.
10. Review with top management.	10. No comparable promotion step.
11. Set the budget, select the advertising vehicles, schedule the buys, and then make the buys.	11. No comparable promotion step.
12. Establish a method for evaluation, arrange for awareness studies, Starch reports, or other research activities.	12. No comparable promotion step.

Even though a company's yearly promotion budget exceeds its advertising expenditures, sales promotion is definitely the stepchild of advertising. Yet sales promotion need *not* be just a cost of doing business; under any circumstances, it can and should be considered an important method for fulfilling marketing goals and strategies.

How should a promotion plan be developed? For our model, let's assume that a company's marketing objectives and strategies have been defined and that its brand is not a new product.

STEP NO. 1

See that the promotion group, whether an internal company department or an outside marketing services agency, is given access to *all* important marketing facts. For everyone involved, this means sharing information on:

Sales trends	Product features
Pricing	Budget constraints
Target market	Legal implications
Consumer attitudes	Profit margins
Sales force	Positioning
Market share	Distribution
Packaging	Company policies
Competition	Media
Advertising and promotion history	

STEP NO. 2

Establish the *year's* overriding promotion goal. This goal should be a broad, clear definition of the role of promotion in the total marketing plan, especially in relation to advertising, product positioning, packaging, and so on. This is the *promotion philosophy* for the brand, discussed in Part II. In this way, promotion can have a definite impact on brand image, or it can help improve the brand's consumer franchise and position, as it does in the cigarette industry.

STEP NO. 3

Determine promotion objectives for the entire year. Since promotion objectives and marketing objectives are interrelated, they should be developed simultaneously. They should also be simple, attainable, and *measurable*. Management cannot evaluate the year's promotions objectively if no one knows what they were designed to accomplish. Without standards of measurement, furthermore, neither the company nor the agency learn from the experience. The entire year's objectives should be similar to the following:

Consumer	Sales Force	Trade/Retail
Encourage trial	Improve knowledge of brand/promotion	Expand distribution
Generate repeat purchases	Improve communication/presentation skills	Obtain special retail price features
Encourage new uses	Attention/support for brand	Gain off-shelf displays
Support advertising	Enthusiasm/motivation	Increase (improve) shelf-space allocation
Improve brand image	Change attitudes toward product	Encourage dealer loading
Increase brand loyalty		Preempt competition

These kinds of objectives are innumerable and limited only by the problems and opportunities facing the product. It is important to note that the above objectives are not complete because they are not measurable. The overall objective may be to increase distribution from 65 percent to 75 percent.

STEP NO. 4

Establish the promotion strategies as they relate to the objectives. Strategies refer to how the company plans to reach its promotion objectives. Typically, separate strategies should be developed for each objective. If the marketing plan calls for the introduction of a new consumer use, for example, the following promotion objectives and strategies might be developed:

Target	Objective	Strategy
Sales force	Generate attention and enthusiasm	Create incentive program
Trade	Gain off-shelf display and special price features	Offer a step-up allowance contingent on off-shelf display
Consumer	Encourage new use	Provide new use ideas

STEP NO. 5

Review the objectives and strategies with management to accomplish the following:

1. An agreement to avoid decision-making changes later in the year (changes can cause havoc with the timing and quality of promotion activity).
2. An agreement to avoid hassles over budgeting.
3. A plan to prevent major blunders down the road, such as conflicts with the manufacturing department over special packaging needs or with the corporate finance group over the proper costing of promotion expenditures.
4. A plan to help management understand how promotion relates to other marketing activities.

STEP NO. 6

Establish the tactics to be used to fulfill the company's promotion objectives and strategies, bearing in mind that any tactics, especially those directed at consumers, should be consolidated with the advertising plan and other marketing directions. Tactics refer to each individual promotion and the actual techniques that will be employed for the consumers, the sales force, and the trade. Basic tactics include:

1. Sampling
2. Coupons
3. Trade coupons
4. Trade allowances
5. Price offs
6. In-, on-, or near-packs
7. Free in-the-mail premiums
8. Self-liquidating mail-ins
9. Contests and sweepstakes
10. Refund offers
11. Bonus packs
12. Stamp and continuity plans

In addition, a promotion technique can be a sales incentive program, a seminar, a new merchandising technique, or a trade relations program. By defining promotion tactics on a simplistic 12-technique basis, creativity is severely restricted.

A second part of step 6 involves setting up a budget. How much will it cost to develop and conduct an incentive program for the sales force? Will it cost too much? If it is too costly, what other alternatives will accomplish the same goal? If objectives are too ambitious, given the potential funding, they may have to be changed or the budget increased.

STEP NO. 7

Establish methods to evaluate the total plan and the components within it. This step is necessarily guided by the way the objectives are stated.

To evaluate the amount of special pricing at retail, a company can review A. C. Nielsen or Burgoyne Index information. If a company's objective is to change sales attitudes, it can conduct special surveys. All efforts require evaluation to determine how successful, or unsuccessful, a program has been. The long-run advantage of this extra expenditure is better performance and credibility down the road.

STEP NO. 8

Write up the plan in total and submit it as part of the brand's *complete* marketing plan.

STEP NO. 9

Begin planning the specific promotion executions.

STEP NO. 10

This is the never-ending phase of follow-through. It includes ensuring that the tactical executions for each promotion period meet the stated objectives and strategies, that the promotions are adequately communicated throughout the channels of distributions, that the inevitable snags and problems get ironed out, that budgets are preserved, and that results are measured.

SUMMARY

These steps help illustrate how the promotion plan *should* be developed. In brief, the steps are as follows:

1. Conduct a market situation review.
2. Define the role of promotion in the total marketing mix.
3. Set the promotion objectives by period for the entire year.
4. Set promotion strategies by period for the entire year.
5. Review the role definition, the promotion objectives, and the promotion strategies with management.
6. Establish the promotion tactics and develop the budget.
7. Determine the methods for evaluating the promotions.
8. Submit the promotion plan as part of the total marketing plan.
9. Begin planning specific executions.
10. Follow through.

Promotion planning alternatives are clear. A company can treat an $8 million promotion budget as 16 $500,000 projects with no clear objectives, separate strategies, or knowledge of the results. Or, with planning, it can accomplish a great deal more.

Let's consider what a totally integrated plan looks like.

THE McDONALD'S MARKETING PLAN, 1979

The McDonald's Marketing Plan for 1979 (made public in February of that year) clearly illustrates the importance McDonald's places on large-scale combining of media and non-media marketing to further the sale of its products (see Figure 22–1).[1]

The company provides two basic aids:

1. A massive budget for advertising, promotion, and public relations at all levels, including a substantial increase in expenditures over previous years. (As an example of a typical increase in budget, McDonald's announced that in 1977 it had spent $160 million on national and local advertising and promotion. McDonald's traditionally ties expenditures to sales; and, since it enjoyed significant increases in sales in 1977 and 1978, the 1979 budget increased accordingly.)

McDONALD'S® 1979

Month/week header: D 25 | JAN 1 8 15 22 29 | FEB 5 12 19 26 | MAR 5 12 19 26 | APR 2 9 16 23 30 | MAY 7 14 21 28 | JUNE 4 11 18 25 | JULY 2 9 16 23 30 | AUG 6 13 20 27 | SEPT 3 10 17 24 | OCT 1 8 15 22 29 | NOV 5 12 19 26 | DEC 3 10 17 24

ADVERTISING PROMOTION

O P N A D

- **ADULT:** ONE & ONLY TASTE | VALUE | BREAKFAST | ADULT CAMPAIGN — BEST CUSTOMER BENEFITS / FAMILIES / INDIVIDUALS | UNIQUE PRODUCT BENEFITS | CHRISTMAS
- ADULT (continued): NATIONAL INTRODUCTION
- **CHILDREN:** HAMBURGER/CHEESEBURGER | BREAKFAST | RONALD McDONALD' CAMPAIGN — DINNER / PRODUCT | CHRISTMAS
- CHILDREN (continued): INTRODUCTION
- **CONTINUITY:** TWEEN, QSCV PRINT, ETHNIC, BREAKFAST
- **PROMOTION RECOMMENDATIONS:** COLORING CALENDAR | VALENTINES | CHEER | SHAMROCK | FLAIR/GAME | KID'S DAY / KID'S DAY / KID'S DAY | HAPPY MEAL™ | 4TH FLAVOR | CONTINUITY GAME | GIFT CERTIFICATE ORNAMENT

L O C A L

- PROMOTION
- ADULT
- CHILDREN

VERTICAL | VERTICAL | INTRODUCTION | VERTICAL | VERTICAL

COMMUNITY MARKETING

N A T I O N A L

- **CREW MOTIVATION:** CREW COMMUNICATION | CREW COMMUNICATION | CREW MOTIVATION
- **LOCAL MARKET OPPORTUNITIES:** WASHINGTON'S & LINCOLN'S BIRTHDAYS, VALUE, BLACK HISTORY | SHAMROCK SHAKE, BREAKFAST EASTER FISH KID'S DAY | MOTHER'S DAY SPANISH SENIORS FLAG DAY FATHER'S DAY | INDEPENDENCE DAY HAPPY MEAL | SUNDAES/SHAKES | LABOR DAY COLUMBUS DAY THANKSGIVING, HALLOWEEN GAME | GIFT CERTIFICATES CHRISTMAS
- **NATIONAL CAL SUPPORT:** HAMBURGER | VALUE | INTRODUCTION | MD / MD / MD
- **OPNAD SUPPORTED-PR:** ONCE UPON A CLASSIC | ALL AMERICAN BASKETBALL | ALL AMERICAN BAND | ALL AM BASKETBALL
- **NON-OPNAD SUPPORTED PR:** RONALD McDONALD HOUSE™ | FILM-EDUCATIONAL MATERIALS | ALL AMERICAN BAND

L O C A L

- CREW MOTIVATION
- LSM
- LSM
- PR

Courtesy of McDonald's Corporation

OPNAD is Operators National Advertising Fund.

2. Competitive activities reports sent to franchises and local agencies containing information about each of McDonald's main competitors' promotion activities.

Changes in the marketing plan each year are based on marketing management's perception of the plan's overall performance in the previous year, its strengths, and any weaknesses in the face of competition. For 1979, therefore, the company decided to affect certain changes again: a more aggressive use of media with advertising concentrated on fewer products or subjects for longer periods than previously; greater attention on certain heavy-user groups (e.g., ethnic, age, and young family); and greater use of fewer, simpler, tested promotions.

Worked out in weekly units, the plan called for effort in the following categories:

> *National advertising*—including network TV (25 percent of total expenditures), local TV, radio, and print media, along three distinct lines of concentration:
>
> *Adults*—product, service, and highlighted events, all main concerns of adults, but divided into alternating phases.
>
> *Children*—largely product and meal-time features, made attractive to children's eating preferences.
>
> *Continuity subjects*—worked into the advertising to adults and children are subjects such as quality-service-cleanliness-value (QSC&V), breakfast, "tween-teen," and ethnic emphasis.
>
> *Promotion recommendations*—all nonmedia programs that are "recommended" because all franchises do not necessarily participate in all promotional programs.
>
> *Vertical promotions*—each of these is of 5 to 6 weeks duration spread throughout the year, and each promotes part(s) of the product line with the help of premiums.
>
> *Supportive promotions*—each lasts 2 to 4 weeks, includes special sale of particular product (e.g., french

fries) or giveaways, and is intended to promote the entire line of products.

Crew motivation—used for internal promotions only, for employee incentive, lasts an average of five weeks.

Community marketing opportunities—a wide array of promotions to tie in with community celebrations which individual franchises might find suitable in their own communities.

Public relations—a variety of planned support involving athletic events, syndicated TV for local participation, educational films, and the famous Ronald McDonald House in Chicago tied in with Children's Memorial Hospital.

CHAPTER 23

Research and Promotion

Promotion testing and research focus on several key questions:

What are the effects of sales promotion on volume, profit, and competitive position of the brand?

How can a brand use sales promotion most effectively?

How can sales promotion be used effectively with other elements of the marketing mix, that is, with advertising, trade deals, and incentives?

What is the optimum advertising/sales promotion ratio?

How do various types of promotion tactics work?

What is the best way to evaluate these tactics?

What are the best media for a given promotion?

Beyond these, there is the fundamental economic question for each tactic, some of which might be:

If we use a coupon, how much should that coupon be?

If we offer a rebate, what should the optimum rebate value be?

If we conduct a sweepstakes or game, how large should the prize pool be?

Only now is the promotion industry beginning to assess these questions with some degree of sophistication. For example, one promotion pretesting program, called ACTION, measures the following:

A **appropriateness**—is this promotion, offer, or tactic appropriate for this company?

C **comprehension**—do the consumer and the trade understand this promotion, and can it be communicated?

T **targeting** to the right market segment. Are we hitting the audience that we hope to hit with this activity?

I **image**—is the promotion consistent with respect to the image of the brand and the advertiser?

O **objectives**—will this promotion achieve the clients' objectives?

N **norms** (the benchmark)—how does this activity compare with the benchmark of other activities in the field?

Some pretesting work such as the ACTION program is being conducted around the country. Many academicians are entering the promotion research arena to develop a predictive model that will tell us how effective a given program will be *before* we actually go into the marketplace. As yet, there is no completely reliable model, but the ACTION system is as good as any currently devised. Even though the ACTION program is only 65 to 70 percent reliable as a predictor, it does provide interesting and helpful diagnostics relative to the creative and the executional plan.

One of the obvious major problems in trying to put together a totally accurate predictive model is that each company is different, each sales organization is different, and the trade's reaction to each sales organization is different. In order to do a reasonably effective job of measuring the predictive success of a promotion, each organization has to develop its own benchmarks, its own set of norms.

Until recently, marketers have been reluctant to spend much in the promotion-testing and evaluation arena, and, as a result, very little is known. Only now are efforts being made to set up a computerized promotion evaluation system by tactic, by type of company, and by type of market. Once established, it will still not be a 100 percent reliable predictor of tactics by category. It will, however, provide a guideline. There are simply too many variables for such a model to accommodate.

What are some of those variables? First, marketers have to ask themselves whether their brand is a major or minor one, and whether it is in a promotion-sensitive/promotion-active category? In other words, for that promotion-prone consumer (on whom there has begun some market research) is the brand in a promotion-prone category? Soft drinks, for example, are in a promotion-prone category. Second is the category of velocity. Is there considerable movement of product, implying high consumption of product? Third, there is the question of whether the brand is in a category of heavy advertising. Is the major brand so strong that the cost of encouraging the consumer to switch is just not affordable? Fourth is the category of frequency, especially promotion frequency. How frequently are products within the category of the brand promoted? Are heavy display features necessary in that category? Fifth is the question of what happens when promotions do occur. What motivates the consumer? Is that motivation a discount? Does the product or its promotion encourage stockpiling?

Variables such as these preclude the practicality of devising a universal and airtight pattern for promotion evaluation. The obvious answer lies in developing the appropriate baseline data similar to those in the ACTION system even though that system is not totally reliable.

What seems to be axiomatic is that the more frequently a brand is promoted, the less frequently the trade participates in the promotion activity of that brand. Conversely, the less frequently a brand or category is promoted, the more likely the trade is to participate when promotions are made available.

A. C. Nielsen research services provide the guidelines by which many manufacturers judge their promotions' effectiveness. But the manner in which the Nielsen research is secured and the inconsistency of the reporting periods relative to the short duration of a promotion seem to indicate that the data is frequently less than ideal for determining a promotion's effectiveness with precision.

However, if it were possible for marketers to ensure the time when Nielsen audits were compiled, and if they were to make their promotions coincide with the audits, the results could approach some semblance of accuracy. This is virtually impossible, obviously, so even Nielsen research, as popular as it is, is less than 100 percent accurate for measuring a promotion activity's effectiveness. Selling Areas Marketing, Inc. might provide more reliable data since it tends to measure warehouse withdrawals and retail inventory rather than just shelf activity; hence, the reporting system is a little broader. For purposes of accurate promotion effectiveness, however, it is debatable.

CHAPTER 24

The Marketing Services Agency and the Client

CONVERSATIONS, PERCEPTIONS

Q. Where do you position a marketing services agency?

A. We are like marketing consultants in that we do evaluations, and we do objective-setting. We devise strategies.

Q. You do not do in-depth research?

A. No, we do not. We try to identify the marketing personality of our client company. For example, let's say Company A is a leader in its industry and Company B isn't. Company A sells through distributors, Company B sells through distributors. They both sell to the same retailers. What's the difference? There is a difference in personality of the two companies. There's a difference in perceived value of their respective products. There's a difference in the brand, in the image, and in the consumer attitude. There's a difference in the way the retailers react to each. There's a difference in the personality of the sales force.

There are differences in corporate personalities. And what we might take for granted for Company A is a big and complicated deal for Company B, which isn't close to Company A in industry reputation.

Q. Does Company B want to be close?

A. Of course. Everyone wants to be close to A. Company B, like any company, wants its products to be perceived as the best value. The marketing management of Company B wants its company to be as important to the retailers as Company A is, but it can't be. It can't be if it attacks a problem on the same basis as Company A. That would be like saying, "Well, tomorrow morning I'm going to take every Chevrolet in the world and make it a Cadillac." You simply cannot do it. You can put all the features and benefits you can think of into the Chevrolet, but it will take years to convince consumers that they can buy a Cadillac-equivalent for half the price. They'll never buy it. Chevrolet says, "We are going to stay right where we are. We happen to be selling a lot more cars than Cadillac sells. Cadillac is more profitable per unit sold, but as a corporation we are more profitable than they are." The field personality and positioning of that company and that product must be understood. The things you do for Cadillac you would not do for Chevrolet.

Q. What do advertising agencies do in greater depth than you?

A. They are far more analytical about consumer issues.

Q. You mean about consumer preference?

A. Yes, consumer preference. They are more analytical. And they will inundate you with reams of material information.

Q. But isn't this consumer-oriented information?

A. It could be consumer-oriented; it could be trade-oriented. It could be anything. The point is that they really dig. Our issue is to get a sense of feel for the personality of the components in our client's business. That's what we are about. Therein lies the difference.

Q. OK, then. When you are talking to a client, do you talk about the necessity of the client understanding himself better by going to your kind of services, to the marketing services agency?

A. Not really. We don't ask him to do that. I mean, we have the capabilities of doing some of this stuff, the talent to analyze, but there are two things the client himself has to learn on his own. He must understand what the distribution system is all about and the influences in that system. And he must understand how the personality that he has created for his product or his brand fits into the needs of the distribution system. He must know where he is positioned relative to the competition so he knows where he is going to go. If I want to get to Philadelphia and I'm already in Philadelphia, maybe I really want to get to Los Angeles.

Q. Does this seem logical to you: after you think the objectives are clear in a promotion, and the client thinks the objectives are clear, and they turn out not to be clear, is it because the client did not seek the kinds of services that your kind of company could give him to make his objectives clearer?

A. That's possible, sometimes. A case in point: we went to work for a laundry supply company, and the client thought what he needed were promotions to move his business. And we went out, did the work, and discovered that the personality the client had envisioned about his company was absolutely inconsistent with what the trade thought. Second, his sales force personnel were not executing what they had to execute. And his operations were not delivering what his operation manuals said they were supposed to be delivering. The client wasn't aware of the problems. He thought everybody was working by the book and that all he had to do was place some promotions on top of everything, and life would be wonderful. When we discovered these things, we went back to the client and said, "Hey, it ain't working out there the way you think it's working. Our recommendation to you is that you fire us immediately and hire a sales manager." And that's what he did.

So, was it a big, deep analytical kind of assignment? No, not at all. But in seeking this "sense of feel," in finding out how his people sold, what the customers thought, and where they fit, we discovered that nothing he thought was *happening* was actually taking place. And it would have been silly for us to develop promotions that had absolutely no chance of working.

Q. What happens when you agree with a client on objectives and the client doesn't agree with your solutions?

A. There's give and take in any business. When that happens, more often than not, the client has rethought what we've agreed on and has not told us. That's why I can't overemphasize the importance of clarifying objectives. We once went through that very kind of experience with a retail company that sells both to department stores and specialty stores. We agreed on a course of action, and we said that we would come up with a solution to the problem for X number of dollars. We then presented our solution to the problem, and the client said, "Wait a minute, that's not what we want." Well, the client was new, and we wanted to make an effort to get along in this new territory. What we *really* wanted to say was, "Fine, but that is the solution to the problem you gave us. Now what you are doing is changing the objective on us, and you want us to go back and do it again for nothing. We're not going to do that because you've changed the ballgame. It's going to cost you more money. You are sending our people back to the drawing board."

Q. What *did* you do?

A. What any company would do in a new situation. We pointed out this additional complication, and we compromised. He gave a little, and we gave a little.

Q. We know that the advertising agency handles media; but what to you seems to be the biggest difference between your kind of agency and the advertising agency?

A. Well, the biggest single difference, theoretically, is that the advertising agency should be doing the same kind of investigative work that we are. They should seek to have this sense of feel for company personality in creating advertising, but I don't think that kind of advertising revolution is just over the horizon. Why, we ask ourselves, waste money on an advertising campaign that promises, figuratively speaking, that Chevrolets fly? Nobody in the world is going to believe it. Even if the best thing that can happen for anybody is that Chevrolets fly, they are *not* going to fly. And nobody would believe that they could.

Q. But the advertising agencies have to do the same kind of thing you do before they start creating advertising. They have to know what's going on out there. Then they have to come up with some creative positioning.

A. Yes, they have to do that. But there are some differences. When we make our credential presentation, we go through an initiation part; we talk about initiation of a project within the agency, and we talk about how an advertising agency has forms the creative people use. The form has a segment where you put the picture, and underneath it a rectangle for the copy. The point is that the strategic decisions are made well in advance of the involvement of the creative people. You know when you begin a project that, if you're in the advertising business and you're a creative person, you are going to make TV commercials or radio commercials or print ads.

   In our business, we don't have forms. Our creative people are going to sit down and deal with the objectives while looking at a blank piece of paper. There isn't going to be anything there. We must put any creative idea through a variety of screens that will say this will work or it won't work.

Q. Let's take a business. How about the beer business? Does advertising in that business take into consideration what the climate is between the marketer and distribution?

A. No. I think the answer is that the advertising agency will not concern itself with this climate. It will not concern itself, as a general rule, with the climate that exists in the distribution channel. It *will* concern itself with the climate of that brand in regard to the consumer.

Q. Should it concern itself here?

A. Yes, marginally, it should, but it's not a big deal.

Q. Is its concern for problems of climate between the marketer and distribution a concern that becomes the cost of doing business for them?

A. That's probably how they look at it. If the advertising is doing a good and believable job, but the product isn't available where and when it should be, the answer to your question is definitely *yes*. If they are concerned about the effectiveness of the advertising, then by definition they have to be concerned with the distribution. But most of the time, they aren't.

Q. What *does* the advertising agency do that you do?

A. It really depends on the agency. The smaller agencies try to do all the things that we do because it's necessary from a revenue standpoint. On the other hand, the larger agencies don't. Their principal concern is with the consumer. And I don't dispute that their contribution is substantial. They *tell* us that their principal concern is the consumer. Usually, what they say to the distributor, or would like to say, is, "If we are doing all this, you're just not doing your job. We are doing a hell of a job here, and you're loafing. You're not getting us the distribution we should have, you've got too many out-of-stocks, you're not in the right locations, you're selling K mart when you should be selling Bloomingdale's."

And what they're saying is generally accurate. We had a situation with an international company that produces a consumer product and that has a licensing division. They have eight or nine licensees, but only one is really successful. And that's because he's selling Montgomery Wards. He's *really* selling them. The rest are living with the licensing agreement that says that they will not sell to chains. They are not able to sell. It's unrealistic to put those kinds of handcuffs on the business.

Q. If I were listening to an advertising agency's pitch to me because I wanted to select an agency, what would I look for?

A. One of the screens would be their ability to understand my distribution. Otherwise, it wouldn't count at all for me because I would say, "You have lots of good creative ideas, but you don't really understand my business."

Q. Does the agency come back and say, "We agree that we don't understand your business, but that is what we do in the process of working together?"

A. You could say that.

Q. They would never say that they don't understand your business?

A. No, but the presentation could communicate that very clearly.

Q. I suppose very discerning advertising/promotion people would see that; but if they weren't discerning, they wouldn't see it.

A. In most cases, that's not quite the situation. That manager might just identify that fact but still say, "We want you to do our advertising. Don't you worry about our distribution. You achieve for us in terms of awareness, image, and consumer attitude what it is we want, and we'll handle the distribution." And the relationship might be positioned that way. That's why the advertising agency does not do what we do. The advertising agency relationship should be a much broader kind of responsibility; but, fortunately for promotion agencies, advertising agencies are not trying to become broader. They say, "We do creative." And I'm not demeaning it; but whenever they get into the areas of distribution, sales organization, motivation, incentives, training, and field communication, they do poorly. They don't give those things the energy that we do. It's not that they don't have the talent; they do.

Q. But you obviously put importance on creativity, too, don't you?

A. Yes, creativity in distribution problems is our stock-in-trade. Ideas are the heart of our creativity. Ideas are what matter—and not necessarily the big splash to convey those ideas. I was once accused in an important trade paper of being a smart aleck when I was asked the best way to communicate a promotion. I said the best way is on a mimeographed sheet of paper. A good promotion almost communicates itself.

I meant it. I wasn't being a smart aleck. And, of course, the person who was doing the interview got very angry with me. For me to say that a 35 mm Hollywood production is the best way to communicate a promotion might be a way to put a lot of people to work and spend a lot of the client's money, but it might be contrary to what is really needed and certainly superfluous to the situation. We'd be right back where we started 20 years ago—selling things. We could certainly generate more revenue that way than by producing a mimeographed sheet of paper, but the idea wouldn't be any better, and that's what should matter to the client. If I can get paid only for the time it takes to put an idea on a mimeographed sheet of paper, then both the client and I are happier, and richer, I might add.

Q. Then are you saying that the simpler the visual representation of an idea the better?

A. No, I'm not saying that at all. I *am* saying that sales promotion has come of age. Our business is helping the client's business, not exploiting it. Ideas are supposed to be action-effective; they are not supposed to exist for their own sake. Besides, times have changed, and people's money and time are harder to come by. There is, or should be, a graphic personality that exists for the brand, and the graphics of promotion should be consistent with the graphic personality of the brand. Also, graphics affect budgets, time, distribution, workable sales tools, and when sale material can be put up.

One subject that came up at a soft drink bottler meeting was a Christmas promotion. The bottlers were saying, "Man, we need a spectacular display for Christmas," and the folks at corporate headquarters were jumping up and down: "Yeah, that's what we need, a spectacular display!" And I said, "OK, people, let me tell you the implications of that. It's going to take your route person or the people in the store 45 minutes just to assemble the display. Can you afford that?" "Are you kidding us?" they asked. "Absolutely not. I recommend that you rethink the whole concept because you are talking about time and you're talking about money." We didn't get into the cost or the biggest point of all—the route person doesn't need it, nor does the retailer.

Q. In promotion activity, what do you mean when you refer to price as a promotion tool?

A. Well, that process involves more than activity just in my business. The obvious answer is that price as a promotion tool means using the price of a product to promote its sale. It's also obvious that a lower price is a promotion tool; but pricing as a promotion tool does not necessarily mean promoting the sale of a product by reducing the price. If a manufacturer can sell a cigarette lighter for $1.50, we assume it's a good price and includes a realistic profit for the trouble of manufacturing it in the first place. What the world does not need, though, is another $1.50 cigarette lighter. Now, if that same lighter could be sold for 69 cents, that would probably be pretty remarkable in the marketplace; but manufacturing costs, under the original conditions, prevent manufacturers from doing that.

What they can do, however, is price that same cigarette lighter at $10.95 and create a special kind of image for it. They can sell the lighter for more by heavy brand image advertising.

Q. What you're saying is that the stronger the brand identification, the more you can charge relative to the competition.

A. Yes, absolutely. The two principal ingredients to good brand image are advertising and packaging.

Q. Then, in other words, brand image building is primarily or exclusively an advertising function? I mean, can *you* promote brand image, or are you simply reinforcing through promotions?

A. We are reinforcing the image through promotion. But the point is that manufacturers not only profit from the advertising, they also profit from the packaging, the pricing, and the promotion. In promotional terms, this is called *impacting* [*impact* as a transitive verb, meaning to force tightly together]. Promotion can impact. Pricing can impact. Distribution can impact.

The image of a product available for sale at K mart is very different from a product for sale at Neiman-Marcus in Dallas or Marshall Field's in Chicago. A person will buy a product from Neiman-Marcus and never bat an eye about paying the Neiman-Marcus price *because* of the brand and *because* of its distribution. There is a certain product quality image inherent to its being in that store.

Q. Is that because of the consumer's feeling of reliability and faith in the retailer?

A. Absolutely. Consumers' faith in the product depends in large measure on their faith in the top quality store to handle a quality product; and that's why distribution can impact image.

The classic story of brilliant strategy in this regard is the Dial Soap story. Dial Soap was originally sold at a very high price in quality retail outlets. It was a specialty soap. The company placed big advertising emphasis on selling Dial to a high-priced group of consumers, and major retailers all over the country bought Dial Soap mostly on the basis of their own ability to advertise and sell it. Rather than go into the marketplace to do battle with all the package goods people on their own ground, the Dial people said, "We will establish an image with this product through heavy advertising with quality department stores." They sold the soap for $1 a bar in an attractive package while they were in the process of building a plant to manufacture in large quantity.

Once the plant was completed, they rushed into volume distribution and, in effect, said, "You can have the famous Dial Soap, folks, three bars for a quarter . . . the same great soap!"

There was a virtual sales explosion, but the image and quality reputation of the product was well-established by going through this very selective distribution and creating for that distribution a very high noise level. All Dial advertisements were tied in with fine department stores, such as Marshall Field's of Chicago, Goldwater's of Scottsdale, Saks Fifth Avenue in several cities, Richard's of Atlanta, or Neiman-Marcus. Dial was perceived as being available at the best stores, in the best departments, beautifully packaged at the cosmetics counter. In later years, the company used saturation advertising, extremely heavy in broadcast and print media. Those who remember the all-pervasive catch-phrase, "Aren't you glad you use Dial? . . ." actually remember Dial advertising when the company went to mass distribution.

PROBLEMS, SOLUTIONS

Solutions are seldom arrived at easily and without careful objective-setting, effective strategy, and creative development. To illustrate how problems are ultimately solved, the following sections discuss typical problems dealt with by the marketing services agency and their final solutions.

Problem. Trying to build additional sales in a business where sales, though generally steady, are made primarily through impulse purchases.

The Wrigley Company has such a problem consistently. In the gum business almost 90 percent of sales are impulse sales. People simply do not preplan to buy chewing gum. This company had planned to market an Olympic promotion, calling its promotional package the Olympak. When the United States boycotted the summer Olympics in Moscow, Wrigley quickly changed it promotion's title to the Sportpak. This self-liquidating premium of an $8.95 backpack presented a good reason to put up four displays *and* counter displays of its 18-stick "planning pack" that normally does not get displayed anywhere in a store.

The whole purpose of this tactic was simply to get displays in parts of the store other than the front end (frequently next to the cash registers). More displays meant more impulse purchases. By simply recognizing buying patterns instead of trying to change them, the Wrigley Company was able to generate greater volume.

Problem. Trying to maintain sales volume continuity in the fast-food business.

Researching McDonald's franchises revealed that children were sharing the "add-on" items to the various hamburger sandwiches—i.e., their french fries and soft drinks. Here was an opportunity to build a *total* family business. So a new theme was developed called "Happy Meal" in six different theme boxes, such as the "Old West Happy Meal." This continuity promotion was designed strictly for children: a regular hamburger, a regular order of fries, a soft drink, and a premium, all put into a box that also contained puzzles and games. Each child would naturally want his or her own

"Happy Meal." The consumer picked up the cost of the premium and the box even though the promotion was built around the standard food products; and though the idea was to be a continuity promotion—that is, to maintain sales volume or build on it—its single problem was its success: the franchises wanted to carry it on their regular menu instead of making it a promotional item.

Problem. Trying to get beer displays in stores and finding the real audience in beer merchandising.

The beer business has certain peculiarities. First, there are 50 state commissions that control promotional guidelines, and breweries operating in those states cannot sell anything directly. Second, distributors are independent of breweries and basically control the acceptability of promotional programs; the individual retail outlets follow their lead. Regardless of the merits or cleverness of a promotion from a brewery standpoint, it must appeal to the distributors. Third, getting beer displays in supermarkets or especially in package liquor stores where space is at a premium can mean as much as an 800 percent increase in sales. Fourth, even the distributor managements are not as important in the decision process as distributor-salespeople, the men who drive the trucks and deliver the beer. This is a very macho audience, and if the promotion is not sufficiently masculine in its appeal, the displays will simply not get set up. Several years ago, The Seven-Up Company learned a tremendously valuable lesson in regard to promotions and distributor-salespeople: it had created a very clever, "really cute," promotional idea, and the drivers hated it.

Miller Brewing Company benefited by Seven-Up's experience. Miller's promotional program tied in with the AAU Boxing Team in an attempt to build some attention around the Olympics. The theme was "Work Out Like a Champ." The premium tie-in was a $6.95 jump rope that boxers use in their workouts. Without having to furnish a proof-of-purchase, consumers could send for the jump rope and an instruction booklet about working out (see Figure 24–1). For the states that wouldn't allow this promotion, Miller simply did a generic promotion that said, in effect, "Miller Supports the U.S. Boxing Team."

FIGURE 24-1

Miller Brewing "Work Out Like a Champ" Boxing Promotion

Courtesy of Miller Brewing Company

Miller did not particularly care whether it liquidated a single jump rope. The promotion was geared to the driver-salespeople, the real audience for the theme. They identified with it and set up the displays. Miller's marketing services agency knew that, if the displays went up, the beer would sell—no matter what the offer was.

Problem. Giving your sales force something to be involved in and to talk about, *and* giving the trade a reason to buy from you rather than from someone else.

Few companies are as successful as The Muppets at addressing this problem. The Muppets Company licenses a variety of merchandise; and the licensed items have become very popular. As a licenser, the company is unique because it does something for its licensees rather than just charge them royalties. It realizes that the more merchandise it can help its licensees sell, the greater its own revenues are going to be.

With the impetus of *The Great Muppet Caper* (see Tactics Introduction, Part III), the Muppets' second movie, and a McDonald's tie-in with drinking glasses (both of which got millions of dollars of media time during June of 1981), the company presented a promotion to department stores called "The Muppet Stuff Boutique." This was a very suitable promotion. Many department stores have "swing areas" on their main floors that they open for promotions. "The Muppet Stuff Boutique" promotion was designed so that the Muppet licensee could gather all Muppet merchandise into one area.

The display material included a backdrop of Kermit and Miss Piggie against which children could have their pictures taken. To promote the sale of merchandise, tandem programs were conducted. A movie ticket stub from *The Great Muppet Caper* enabled a purchaser to get a discount on merchandise. In popcorn given away for every piece of Muppet merchandise purchased, the buyer got a puzzle piece to fit into a display puzzle, and he or she could win prizes this way, too.

Among the cities where the promotion was conducted were Chicago and New York; in both cities, department stores provided both outside and inside windows to draw consumers to the centralized area where all the "Muppet Stuff" merchandise was displayed.

Problem. Trying to increase sales of a small brand by giving the retailer a reason for displaying it.

Large companies that easily sell their big brands sometimes have difficulty selling their small brands (which ordinarily are not displayed with the big ones). Armour & Company (maker of Dial Soap) had just such a difficulty. They have no trouble selling canned meats or Dial Soap; but Parson's Ammonia is a small commodity brand of Armour, and ammonia is no different from other brands.

Armour traditionally offered a 50-cent case allowance to the trade. The trade would not buy more than they normally planned to buy and, allegedly, would put the 50 cents in their pockets. This is a process of "dealing," and, as often happens, manufacturers deal but don't get anything for their deals. The money becomes a bribe, a commonplace occurrence.

Armour then built a promotion around Parson's Ammonia

that required four feet of selling space but made the idea valuable to the retailers: a household cleaning center that enabled retailers to organize all their high-impulse as well as high-profit items (such as buckets, brooms, mops, and sponges) in a display around Parson's Ammonia. It was a 10-case display, which, though only up for a week or two, gave retailers a reason to promote Armour's product.

Promotions for Dial Soap, the number 1 brand, usually amount to 35,000 to 40,000 displays nationally. The Parson's Ammonia promotion consisted of 4,000 erected displays (or 40,000 cases), but that was 4,000 more than the company ever got up before.

Problem.   Helping Kodak compete in a product area where it had never competed before.

It seems to many that Eastman Kodak Company's idea of a promotion is to hang up a sign. Kodak has enjoyed an international reputation for its photographic products and meets virtually no real competition. When it entered the *instant* business with an instant camera, however, it met stiff competition from the Boston-based Polaroid Company.

A promotion was developed for Kodak called "Do A Double Take." A complete promotion that helped all levels of sales, it essentially involved a manufacturer's refund promotion. Consumers could get a refund of up to $20 depending on the camera model they purchased.

Marketing people have learned that the instant camera business is unique in the photographic industry. Unless the film is in the consumer's hands, an instant camera simply does not get used. And since instant cameras are used for fun photography, purchasing film or carrying the camera may easily be postponed. Moreover, the instant business is a captive system—instant camera owners know that Polaroid cameras use only Polaroid film and Kodak cameras use only Kodak film. The object, therefore, was to stimulate the purchase of Kodak film along with sale of Kodak instant cameras.

When consumers received their cash refunds of up to $20, they were also introduced to a film rebate program—a series of 10 redeemable $1 coupons on Kodak instant film, to be redeemed with proof of purchase in groups of three coupons, then three more, and then the final four. A "double take" contest was conceived for the Kodak sales force. If sales reps made their local goals in sales, they could win double prizes, such as double calculators, double lamps, and double tools. If they made their district sales goals, they were awarded bigger double prizes—double watches and double televisions. If they became national sales winners, they could select double sailboats and double vacation trips.

Until this promotion, Eastman Kodak Company had never had a selling contest. The sales force responded very enthusiastically. Results were quite successful because, for the first time, the sales force had something to sell. The promotion gave something to the trade, too, as well as to the consumer. The basic reason for the promotion's success was that it provided motivation to all concerned, from the company to the consumer; it was a complete program.

Problem.   How to develop a promotion that motivates company employees but doesn't give them anything.

When the sale of telephone instruments was deregulated, telephone companies in the United States found themselves on the threshold of a brand new competitive environment. Consumers no longer had to turn to their local telephone companies to buy telephone instruments. Instead, they could buy them from K mart or through catalog houses provided the instruments were registered with the FCC.

When a marketing services agency approached South Central Bell out of Birmingham, Alabama (the first of nine companies the agency worked for) and suggested that its own broad experience in retailing could be of help to them in maintaining their strong position in the telephone instrument business, South Central Bell accepted the help.

South Central Bell (covering Alabama, Kentucky, Louisiana, Mississippi and Tennessee) had, in fact, three channels of distribution from which it was selling (1) the phone-center store employees, (2) the installation and maintenance people (who had the advantage of being able to approach people in the comfort of their homes), and (3) the record office people whom customers call to discuss a billing problem or place an order for telephone service.

The new competitive environment presented a promising situation for the marketing services agency. The agency proposed a "classical" sales incentive program to reward employees according to what they sold. They could win prizes and cash. South Central Bell had to reject the proposal because the company's union contract did not allow any kind of special remuneration to employees.

The program that was finally developed and approved by the company capitalized on the familiar theme, "Reach Out and Touch Someone." It was called the "Reach-Out Relays," a sales contest built over a three-month period (see Figure 24–2).

At the heart of the promotion was a plan to group the sales organization into teams—the phone-center store employees constituted a team, the installation and maintenance crew became a team, and the people in the records office became a team. To each team the promotion said, in effect, "Team,

---

FIGURE 24–2

South Central Bell "Reach-Out Relays" Sales Contest

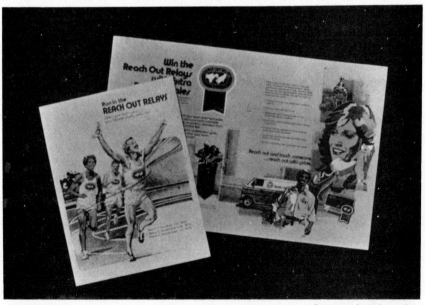

Courtesy of South Central Bell

choose your favorite local charity, and if you reach out for premium sales, you can reach out and truly touch somebody."

The promotional theme was "Reach Out for Sales and Reach Out and Touch Someone." If a team achieved the first month's goal, it could donate $20 to a charity; the second month's goal, $50; and the third month's goal, $100.

The promotion was very important to such local organizations as the Boy Scout troup and the library. It generated peer pressure everywhere, people became involved, absenteeism fell off sharply, and telephone sales increased 24 percent over the same period the previous year. Significant, too, was that the marketing services agency then developed similar phone-center store programs for nine other operating companies because they all had the same problem.

Problem. How to promote selectively; that is, how to develop a promotion by market segmentation.

When McDonald's decided to introduce breakfast as one of its food features, it realized that it had to overcome three major obstacles to be successful, and all had to do with adult eating habits. First, to many people, eating breakfast in a restaurant that primarily sold hamburgers was not like eating breakfast. Second, breakfast eaters are creatures of habit—they eat in the same place, at home or in the same restaurant, breakfast after breakfast, or they do not eat at all. Third, they are largely solitary eaters—they are social loners in the morning.

The object, then, since McDonald's felt that it had the best-tasting quality product of the day, was to try to break that mold. So McDonald's developed what might best be described as an adult bribery promotion. If consumers could be convinced to try McDonald's breakfast, they would become repeat customers. That's what happened.

The promotion was called, "Start Your Morning with a Flair." McDonald's gave away a free 99-cent Flair pen to customers who tried a breakfast item. It altered this idea by offering a Gillette "Good News Razor" with the theme of "Good News in the Morning." In both cases, the company successfully built a breakfast business, different from the lunch business, and did so by developing adult promotions.

The next phase will be for McDonald's to develop a dinner program. In the same store, the promotional programs may involve different products for different parts of the day for different customers, a daily promotional activity.

Problem. How to enable a company that sells a popular candy year-round to remain competitive with specialty candies promoted and sold heavily only during holiday seasons.

Mars, Inc.'s M&Ms is the number 1 selling candy in America. During the Thanksgiving holidays in 1974, however, M&M/Mars found itself temporarily out of business when the supermarket trade began to handle specialty candies, candy canes, chocolate Santa Clauses, bells, and other delectable morsels. The trade bought these specialty candies because they offered a greater profit incentive; but taking on another inventory, especially for a limited period, has inherent problems—often a supermarket does not purchase enough and runs out of stock before it wants to, or it purchases far too much. On December 26, chocolate Santas must be marked down substantially, and profit dwindles.

The object, then, was to design a program to circumvent these problems. "Bake and Make" was that program. It said to the consumer, "Here's how you can use M&Ms around the holidays." Recipes and decoration ideas were placed at the point-of-sale; the same hints and ideas were offered in women's service books. Consumers began to bake with M&Ms and decorate with M&Ms.

To the supermarkets, the program said that, since M&Ms was their number 1 candy, they could take unsold packages off the displays after the holidays and put them back on the shelves—they couldn't lose.

By 1982 the "Bake and Make" holiday promotion was into its eighth year.

Problem. How to support strong brand image advertising, address the right audience in doing so, and help consumers realize that what they see on television or hear on the radio pays off at the store.

For years during the summer, Löwenbräu TV commercials showed a group of happy people on the beach or at a clambake enjoying lobsters and Löwenbräu (one of Miller Brewing Company's brands). Tied in with this advertising was a

FIGURE 24-3

Löwenbräu Premium Promotion

Courtesy of Miller Brewing Company

$96 self-liquidating premium—six live Maine lobsters, 1½ pounds of clams, a large bucket to cook them in, and a booklet suggesting how to prepare and cook them (see Figure 24-3).

Whether the company liquidated a single premium was not as important as the larger purpose, which was to ask both the trade and the consumers, "Who but Löwenbräu, a super premium beer, could offer a promotion and premium like this?"

A postpromotion evaluation revealed that Löwenbräu moved 300 premiums, but the majority of them went to

Löwenbräu distributors who buy directly from the factory. The brewery itself could not run any kind of promotion, but the distributors could, so they ran the promotion for their own buyers.

Was this a successful promotion? It was very successful because it promoted the image of the brand and it supported the company's advertising. Once again, you have to know what the objectives are. It is an outmoded idea that a promotion's success depends on how many premiums you sell or give away.

Problem. How to introduce a new product in an environment of high product failure.

Approximately five of every six new products never achieve the success hoped for by their manufacturer and advertisers. This failure rate touches even big consumer product companies like Procter & Gamble and Kellogg. The primary reason for this failure is too much parity among all products. Appropriate and effective promotion is critically important.

When Warner Lambert and Lifesaver introduced soft bubble gum, William Wrigley, a very conservative company, insisted that the whole idea was a fad, that the entire effort would be a flash in the pan, "We are not going to do this," Wrigley declared.

Soft bubble gum, however, became a half-billion-dollar business, and the Wrigley Company, which did enter the market, found itself the third entry. It caught up rather quickly, nevertheless, and promotion of Wrigley's product contributed substantially to that success.

Hubba Bubba chewing gum, Wrigley's soft bubble gum product, offered an attractive difference: it did not stick to the chewers' hair or face when they blew bubbles. To reinforce the media power, Wrigley's advertising agency developed a trade character for its product called the Gumfighter. The marketing services agency used the trade character in a continuity program to encourage consumers' brand loyalty. Brand loyalty is important in this business because consumers tend to switch brands frequently.

The promotion was geared to children. Each child who mailed six labels to the company received a free premium called the Gumfighters Kit. The kit itself was a paper pre-

FIGURE 24-4

Gumfighters Kit® Game Premium from Wrigley[1]

Courtesy of Wm. Wrigley Jr. Co.

mium—a Gum Holster, a Bubble Meter for bubble-measuring, and a bubble-blowing game complete with spinner—all geared to get children involved with the product (see Figure 24-4).

Added to the Gumfighter program was a Gum Seller's Kit for the sales force to take to the trade. The more gum the trade bought, the more it qualified for adult-type premiums, such as boots, shirts, and saddles.

Mr. Wrigley liked the promotion so well that he gave Gumfighter Kits to those who attended the stockholders' meeting. Since that time the company has sent out over a quarter of a million Gumfighters Kits.

Problem. How to promote a high-tech product successfully after its first introduction by the manufacturer failed.

AT&T, through its operating company, Mountain Bell, introduced a new telephone called the Touch-A-Matic S. This high-tech product was a battery-operated automatic dialer handset that had a peculiarly high-pitched ring. It didn't sell. The marketing services agency, which was asked to solve the problem discovered that the product died primarily because salespeople in phone-center stores were afraid of it. They didn't show it or demonstrate it. Yet consumers needed hands-on experience with the product to be convinced of its potential, for it was an impressive innovation in telephoning.

As a first step, the telephone was renamed, the *Talk of Tomorrow*. From this was created a "Talk of Tomorrow Sweepstakes;" people who won the sweepstakes qualified for high-technology prizes. When a person came into a phone-center store, phone representatives were instructed to ask him to enter this exciting sweepstakes. To enter, the person called a friend, programmed a telephone, *and* entered that friend into the sweepstakes, too. By entering the friend's telephone number and by programming the telephone accordingly, the entrant got the necessary hands-on experience. If he won a prize in the sweepstakes, his friend won a duplicate prize, and the phone-center representative won a prize, too. Everybody had a chance of winning.

The promotion was extremely well-received by Mountain Bell employees and their customers. In the promotion's first six weeks, the company made its first six months of forecasted sales. Since that time, the promotion has been introduced to various other operating companies of AT&T with similar success.

CHAPTER 25

The Corporate Promotion Organization: Structure and Personnel

Although the amount of money being invested in promotion has grown markedly over the last decade, there has been relatively little change in the way companies manage the promotion function.[1]

During the 1980–81 recession, companies reduced staff and levels of management or pushed decision-making authority down to operating units or divisions.

There are no clear-cut preferred methods for managing the promotion function within a company. The promotion function generally seems to be positioned much as the advertising function is. Because organizational charts vary from company to company, so does promotion management.

At Procter & Gamble—which manages its promotion function in relatively the same way since Ralph Glendenning left the company in 1960 to form his sales promotion consulting business—the essential control of promotion rests with a brand assistant, probably the newest person to the brand group. Along with the assistant brand manager who handles advertising, the brand assistant reports to the brand manager.

The brand assistant has dotted-line contact with the promotion development department, which has specialists in such tactics as coupons, point-of-sale, or premiums. In addition, a staff specialist in charge of trade relations provides substantial input in trade deal and allowance policy.

Each brand group writes an annual brand promotion plan, and gathers data from sales, promotion development, advertising, and the brand's advertising agency. P&G rarely uses sales promotion or marketing services agencies in the planning process. Staff specialists contact these sources and other promotion vendors for ideas and implementation skills.

Most companies that have a brand manager system have adapted the P&G approach to promotion management. In other companies, however, promotion specialists may have more or less control over the planning and implementation cycles. Some companies have a strict policy against brand groups dealing with outside agencies or vendors; other companies encourage brand managers to plan, create, and implement promotions directly with outside vendors, just as they deal with ad agencies.

In the early 1980s, Colgate-Palmolive and a few others reorganized themselves along strategic business lines rather than along brand lines. In this type of organization, the promotion staff specialist reports to the group director of product strategy, who is responsible for tactical implementation of long-term strategies and accountable for contributory goals of the business unit's programs.

As a result, some promotion managers in these organizations changed from typically short-range planning to planning in 4-, 5-, or even 12-year time frames. Traditional promotion management does not plan this far in advance.

According to a 1978 study of promotion departments done by the Association of National Advertisers, the promotion department fits into the organization by either reporting to sales advertising or by reporting, under its own banner, to the chief marketing officer. More and more companies have adapted the latter option, principally because of increased promotion investment and the growth of such specialities as

Promotion Management by Brand

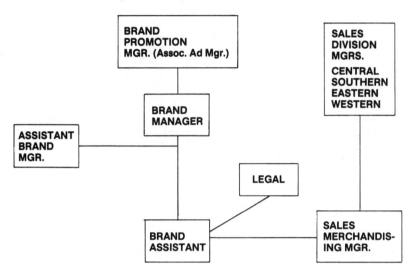

coupon management, premium development, group promotions, sales training, and trade shows.

There are two main variations in promotion management—one has a service orientation with functional specialists, and the other has a planning and development orientation.

In the service orientation, there are specialists in couponing, direct mail, premiums, creative, trade shows, and point-of-purchase. Each specialist reports directly to the executive in charge of promotion within the company. The department is charged with the responsibilities of planning and implementing programs for the company's products or services on a demand basis.

Companies with divisions may elect to locate the promotion department at the corporate level, at the divisional or unit level, or at both levels. General Motors, for example, has a small corporate sales promotion department responsible for multidivisional efforts or special programs such as dealer incentive contests, but each of its divisions has a sizable staff of promotional specialists who have only dotted-line contact with the corporate sales promotion department. In addition, GM has sizable in-house specialist units, such as sales training, that operate autonomously within the corporation but can be used by the divisions.

Planning & Development Orientation

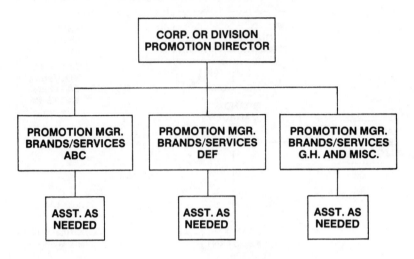

Service Orientation

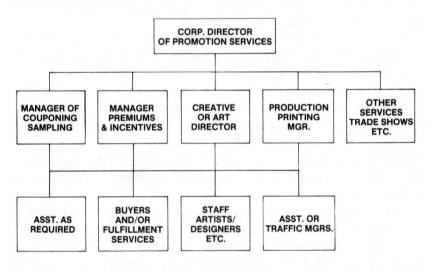

One of the pitfalls of having separate specialists along functional lines, according to some, is that the brand manager or the person responsible for implementing promotional programs has to "shop" or plan programs among the cast of experts. In some companies, this can mean that promotion planning is given short shrift.

The second type of promotion department is organized

along brand or business units, with promotion function personnel matched in tandem with other management resources, such as those from brand, research, sales, and advertising. Promotion development and implementation are managed at the operational level, typically putting brand and promotion together.

Training of promotion development personnel is a corporate responsibility. Also at the corporate level are tactical specialists and other data resources. General Foods pioneered the development of this type of organization, hiring new college graduates into the function and offering a career path that advances to different management levels among different business groups.

The ANA study of mostly large consumer goods companies found that 45 percent of the respondents had marketing services departments supervising the promotion function; 14 percent reported that the advertising department handled promotion; 8 percent said the product manager was responsible for all phases of promotion; and 6 percent said the sales department was responsible for promotion. The balance had no response.

The study also found that 65 percent had a central department for all brands or divisions, 11 percent had brand or divisional departments, and 14 percent had no internal department at all. The balance did not answer.

In addition, 9 percent of the respondents said that they relied primarily on outside sales promotion agencies, and 6 percent said that they relied on their ad agencies for all phases of promotion management.

In his book *The Promotion Planning Process,* Dr. Roger Strang found greater involvement by senior management in the promotional process as expenditures increased. He concluded, however, that the promotion planner, typically a product manager with relatively little experience in promotion and relatively little time to develop and implement effective programs, was enjoying less freedom as a promotion planner as a result of greater top management interest.

Dr. Strang commented that setting promotion objectives, setting budgets, and planning and using inside and outside specialists were the lead problems facing companies. He said that promotion management had been virtually ignored even though companies were investing more in promotion.

NOTES

Chapter 1

[1]Estimates vary slightly on this because of disagreements on the allocation of promotion advertising. This amount emanates from a 1979 Donnelley survey, as reported by several authorities.

[2]Depending on the source, estimates tend to vary from $5 to $10 billion dollars.

[3]For a detailed discussion of decentralization, see John Naisbitt, "From Centralization to Decentralization," in *Megatrends: Ten New Directions Transforming Our Lives* (New York: Warner Books, 1982), pp. 97–129.

[4]*Fortune*, November 8, 1979. There have been more increases since then.

[5]*The Wall Street Journal*, April 4, 1980.

[6]The comments in this section have been extracted from a speech given by Peter K. Francese, publisher of *American Demographics*, at a 1980 sales promotion seminar in Chicago. The statistics have been updated by Mr. Francese to 1985.

[7]For a compelling discussion of U.S. population shifts, see John Naisbitt, "From North to South," in *Megatrends: Ten New Directions Transforming Our Lives* (New York: Warner Books, 1982), pp. 207–29.

Chapter 2

[1]Ovid Riso, ed., *The Dartnell Sales Promotion Handbook*, 6th ed. (Chicago: Dartnell Corporation, 1973), pp. 36–37.

[2]Joseph J. Schroeder, Jr., ed., *Sears, Roebuck & Co. 1908 Catalogue No. 117: The Great Price Maker* (Chicago: Follett Publishing, 1969), viii-ix (Introduction).

[3]Russell D. Bowman, "Merchandising and Promotion Grow Big in Marketing World; Investments Boom," *Advertising Age*, December 30, 1974, p. 21.

[4]Ibid.

[5]Ibid.

[6]Louis J. Haugh, "Agencies Trending toward More Promotion Work, Four A's Finds," *Advertising Age*, July 8, 1974, p. 20.

[7]Ibid., pp. 20, 23.

[8]Tom Dillon, "Markets Are Customer Problems, Not Geography or Demographics," as reported in *Advertising Age*, September 2, 1974, p. 29.

[9]Riso, *The Dartnell Sales Promotion Handbook*, pp. 24–25.

[10]Haugh, "Agencies Trending," p. 20.

[11]Roger A. Strang, "Sales Promotion—Fast Growth, Faulty Management," *Harvard Business Review*, July-August 1976, pp. 115–24.

[12]Ibid., p. 115.

[13]Ibid.

[14]Ibid. For this ratio information, Strang cites Richard J. Weber, "How

Trade Allowances Are Making Mincemeat Out of Profit Objectives" (New York: Association of National Advertisers Financial Management Workshop, 1973).

[15] Strang, "Sales Promotion," p. 117.

[16] Ibid.

[17] Ibid.

[18] Ibid.

[19] Ibid., p. 118.

[20] Ibid.

[21] Ibid.

[22] Ibid., p. 119.

[23] Ibid.

[24] Ibid.

[25] These are matters the interested reader may pursue individually by a thorough study of the report. It can be seen, however, that these recommendations grew directly from what Strang saw as obvious symptoms of neglect of promotion's importance.

[26] Strang, "Sales Promotion."

[27] Robert M. Prentice, "How to Split Your Marketing Funds between Advertising and Promotion," *Advertising Age*, January 10, 1977, p. 41.

[28] Ibid.

[29] Ibid.

[30] Ibid.

[31] As reported in Fred L. Lemont, "Room at the Top in Promotion," *Advertising Age*, March 23, 1981, p. 61.

[32] Ibid.

[33] Ibid.

[34] Ibid.

Chapter 3

[1] The reader might deduce from the explanation that follows that, because some distribution channels are more involved than others, the geometric figure should be other than a triangle. For the sake of simplicity only, we have selected a triangle instead of, for example, a hexagon or octagon.

Chapter 5

[1] Robert M. Prentice, "Proper Ad/Promotion Mix: The Key to Success or Failure," *Sales Promotion Monitor* 1, no. 6 (October 1983), p. 44.

[2] Ibid.

[3] Ibid.

[4] Ibid.

[5] Ibid.

Chapter 6

[1]William T. Moran, "The Advertising Promotion Balance," *Association of National Advertisers Workshop*, April 4, 1978, p. 58. Also see Eugene R. Beem, and H. Jay Shaffer, "Triggers to Customer Action—Some Elements in a Theory of Promotional Inducement," *Marketing Science Institute Research Program Working Paper* (Cambridge, Mass.: Marketing Science Institute, 1981), p. 34.

Chapter 13

[1]In all the negotiations with J. Hensen & Associates, the agency was never permitted to promote the Muppets but was granted all kinds of latitude to promote the movie *The Great Muppet Caper.*

Chapter 14

[1]See *Sales Promotion Monitor,* March 1985.
[2]In-pack and on-pack couponing are clearly the highest redemption rate methods of distribution largely because the consumer has the tendency to purchase that product and will use the coupon to repurchase.

Chapter 18

[1]The following is a partial list of sources helpful in the discussion of tie-in/group promotions: American Association of Advertising Agencies, *Sales Promotion Techniques* (New York, 1978); Louis J. Haugh, "How Group Promos Work," *Advertising Age*, April 27, 1981, p. 56; C. Martin Abbott, "Two Could Be More Mighty than Just One in Promotions," *Advertising Age*, May 5, 1980, pp. S21–S23; "Major Findings Group Promotions Study," The Westport Marketing Group, Inc. (Westport, Conn.: January, 1980), pp. 1–2, 4–7; Cara S. Trager, "Cross-Merchandising Charges Duracell Batteries," *Advertising Age*, May 2, 1985, p. 17.

Chapter 22

[1]Reprinted by permission of the McDonald Corporation.

Chapter 24

[1]Gumfighters Kit and Hubba Bubba are registered trademarks of Wm. Wrigley Jr. Company. Reproduced with permission of Wm. Wrigley Jr. Company.

Chapter 25

[1]The material in this chapter, contributed by Louis J. Haugh, originally appeared in slightly different form under his byline in *Advertising Age*, February 1, 1982.

Index